COUNTRIES OF THE WORLD

Nigeria

Gareth Stevens Publishing
A WORLD ALMANAC EDUCATION GROUP COMPANY

About the Author: Yinka Ismail obtained her bachelor of science degree in Geography from Strathclyde University in Glasgow, Scotland. She then went on to obtain her master in philosophy in land management from Reading University, England. She lives and works in Lagos.

Written by
YINKA ISMAIL

Edited by
PAUL ROZARIO

Edited in the U.S. by
**PATRICIA LANTIER
MONICA RAUSCH**

Designed by
LYNN CHIN

Picture research by
SUSAN JANE MANUEL

First published in North America in 2001 by
Gareth Stevens Publishing
A World Almanac Education Group Company
330 West Olive Street, Suite 100
Milwaukee, Wisconsin 53212 USA

Please visit our web site at:
www.garethstevens.com
For a free color catalog describing
Gareth Stevens' list of high-quality books
and multimedia programs, call
1-800-542-2595 (USA) or
1-800-461-9120 (CANADA).
Gareth Stevens Publishing's
Fax: (414) 332-3567.

© **TIMES MEDIA PRIVATE LIMITED 2001**
Originated and designed by
Times Editions
an imprint of Times Media Private Limited
Times Centre, 1 New Industrial Road
Singapore 536196
http://www.timesone.com.sg/te

Library of Congress Cataloging-in-Publication Data
Ismail, Yinka.
Nigeria / by Yinka Ismail.
p. cm. — (Countries of the world)
Includes bibliographical references and index.
ISBN 0-8368-2337-0 (lib. bdg.)
1. Nigeria — Juvenile literature. I. Title. II. Countries of the world
(Milwaukee, Wis.)
DT515.22 .I85   2001
966.9—dc21   2001020232

Printed in Malaysia

1 2 3 4 5 6 7 8 9 05 04 03 02 01

Contents

AN OVERVIEW OF NIGERIA

The Federal Republic of Nigeria has the largest population on the African continent and is sometimes referred to as "the Giant of Africa." Nigeria's geographical landscape is diverse, ranging from the humid swamps of the Niger Delta to the remote, semiarid plains of the north. Such variation in terrain results in a remarkable diversity of plant and animal life. With over 250 ethnic groups, Nigeria's cultural landscape is equally rich and diverse. Blessed with an abundance of natural resources, including oil, Nigeria has a steadily growing economy. Since achieving independence from Britain in 1960, the country has had civil war and many dictators. Nigerians, however, have faith in their recently elected democratic government.

Opposite: **Dressed in traditional clothes, a Nigerian man takes part in a Muslim religious festival in the town of Katsina, northern Nigeria.**

Below: **The central mosque in Kano rises high above other structures in the surrounding area.**

THE FLAG OF NIGERIA

The Nigerian flag is composed of three vertical panels of equal size. The two outer panels are green, representing Nigerian agriculture. The middle panel is white and symbolizes unity and peace. The flag was designed in 1958 by Taiwo Akinkunmi, a student from Ibadan. His design was chosen from over two thousand entries sent in as part of a competition for the best flag design. The flag did not become Nigeria's official flag until October 1, 1960, when Nigeria became independent from Britain. The flag is officially called the Nigerian National and Merchant Flag and Jack.

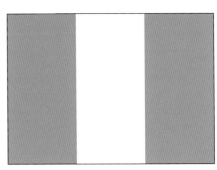

Geography

The Land

Nigeria occupies a land area measuring 356,700 square miles (923,853 square kilometers). The fourteenth largest country on the African continent, Nigeria is the most heavily populated African nation. Nigeria is bordered by Niger to the north, Cameroon and Chad to the east, Benin to the west, and the Gulf of Guinea and the South Atlantic Ocean to the south.

Rich in Rivers

A land of many rivers, Nigeria was named after its major river, the Niger. The Niger River is 2,600 miles (4,183 km) long and is Africa's third longest river. Rising in the highlands of Guinea, the river flows through Guinea, Mali, and Niger, before entering Nigeria from the northwest. The waters continue southward to meet the Benue River at the town of Lokoja. From here, the Niger flows farther south and drains into the Gulf of Guinea in the South Atlantic Ocean through the Niger Delta, a large fan-shaped delta that covers an area of 14,000 square miles (36,260 square km).

The Niger is a source of hydroelectricity and water for irrigation. The river is also a means of transportation.

POLLUTION IN THE DELTA

The Niger Delta along Nigeria's southern coastline supports many plants and animals. The region is also the center of oil exploration and production in Nigeria. The fragile ecosystem of the delta has come under increasing threat from pollution caused by the oil industry.
(*A Closer Look*, page 60)

Below: Passengers wait to disembark from ferries on the Niger River near Onitsha.

Terrain and Vegetation

Nigeria's terrain and vegetation can be divided into four groups. Along the coast is the swampy Niger Delta, home to mangrove trees of the *Rhizophorae* family. These trees have tall roots that grow above ground. The mangrove swamps of the Niger Delta support a thriving ecosystem of plants, fish, and insects.

Immediately north of the swamps is a belt of lush, tropical rain forest, supporting hardwood trees, such as ebony, mahogany, and teak. This region is also rich in oil palm, rubber, and cocoa trees, all of which were major cash crops before the discovery of oil. Logging, subsistence agriculture, and human settlement continue to cause massive deforestation in this area.

North of the forest belt are open grasslands, called savannas, dotted with the occasional tree. Farther north, the long grasses give way to a semiarid region called the Sahel, where acacia and baobab trees thrive. The young leaves of the baobab are edible, while the bark is used for making twine; its large canopy provides shade. The extreme northern part of the country is semidesert and borders the Sahara Desert. Hardly any vegetation survives in the desert sands.

Important highland areas in Nigeria include the Jos Plateau in central Nigeria and the Oban Hills near the southern border with Cameroon. The tallest mountain in the country is Chappal Waddi, which rises 7,936 feet (2,419 meters) in eastern Nigeria.

Above: The dry savannas around Lake Chad in northeastern Nigeria are home to many nomadic tribes.

RICH PLANT LIFE

Nigeria has many plant species. Tropical flowers include bougainvillea and orchids. A large variety of fruit is cultivated in Nigeria, ranging from bananas (*below*) to papayas and mangoes.

Seasons

Situated between the equator and the Tropic of Cancer, Nigeria has a hot, tropical climate. Regional variations in temperature depend on the amount of rainfall each region receives.

In the north, the climate is hot and dry, with one long rainy season from mid-May to September. The hottest months of the year are April and May, when temperatures can reach 100° Fahrenheit (38° Celsius). Annual rainfall in the remote northern reaches can be as little as 20 inches (51 centimeters).

At an average elevation of 4,200 feet (1,280 m) above sea level, the Jos Plateau in central Nigeria experiences the lowest temperatures and lowest humidity of any part of the country. Rainfall here is about 50 inches (127 cm) per year.

Southern Nigeria is warm but not as hot as the north. Along the coastal regions, rainfall is heavy and humidity is very high, although temperatures remain more or less constant throughout the year, at about 90° F (32° C). The rainy season in the south lasts from March to November.

Another factor that determines climate in Nigeria is wind current. The harmattan is a hot, dry, dust-bearing wind that sweeps down from the Sahara onto the plains of the Sahel for about five months a year, between November and March. The winds also reach the coast, but do not blow for more than two weeks in this part of Nigeria.

Below: **A cyclist in Kaduna pedals through the dusty harmattan wind.**

Left: **Visitors to Nigeria's northern savannas may be lucky enough to see animals in the wild. Most animals, however, including the zebras shown here, are found only in Nigeria's many national parks.**

Wildlife

Nigeria's diverse vegetation supports a wide variety of animal life. Lions, giraffes, camels, zebras, and antelope roam the savannas. The tropical rain forests are home to the forest elephant, colobus monkey, giant forest hog, and leopard, as well as many smaller animals, such as the mongoose and anteater. Bird species include the Ibadan weaver bird, which is indigenous to Nigeria. An animal endemic to Nigeria is Sclater's red-eared monkey. The country's rivers teem with crocodiles and many varieties of fish.

Many animals, such as the pygmy hippopotamus and the forest elephant, are endangered. Some animals, such as antelope, hares, snakes, and monkeys, are considered delicacies in Nigeria.

A number of national parks and reserves preserve Nigeria's threatened biodiversity. The most famous is the Yankari National Park, which is home to more than fifty species of mammals, including lions, horned waterbucks, bush bucks, buffaloes, elephants, and baboons. The park also is home to more than 350 species of birds, including many migratory species. Much of Nigeria's wildlife can no longer be seen outside these protected national parks.

PRECIOUS FORESTS

Ninety percent of Nigeria's forest cover has been lost due to indiscriminate logging over the last forty years. One of the few remaining areas of primary tropical rain forest is the Omo Forest Reserve in Ogun State, north of Lagos.

(A Closer Look, page 62)

SAVING THE LOWLAND GORILLA

Parts of eastern Nigeria support tiny communities of one of the world's most endangered primates — the elusive western lowland gorilla.

(A Closer Look, page 64)

History

Prehistory

Human occupation of Nigeria goes back 40,000 years. The oldest human skeleton found by archaeologists in present-day Nigeria has been dated to 9,000 B.C. Historians generally believe, however, that the earliest organized societies in Nigeria were those of the Nok civilization, which flourished between 500 B.C. and A.D. 200.

Kingdoms of the Northern Savanna

The empire of Kanem-Bornu developed near Lake Chad in northeastern Nigeria. One of the most important kingdoms of Nigeria, Kanem-Bornu ruled for 1,000 years, from the ninth to the nineteenth centuries. The kingdom's wealth was based on the trans-Saharan trade: foreign goods from across the Sahara Desert, such as horses, salt, and copper, were exchanged at busy markets for kola nuts and ivory. Islam was also introduced into the empire in the eleventh century through this trade. Trade routes from Kanem-Bornu extended as far north as the Mediterranean Sea.

NOK CULTURE

In 1928, tin miners digging in the town of Nok discovered a series of terra-cotta figurines. These finds revealed evidence of the earliest organized society in Nigeria.
(A Closer Look, page 56)

Below: Kano was one of the northern cities that grew rich from trans-Saharan trade. Kano State has a history dating back to the tenth century.

The Islamic Hausa states began to establish themselves in about the tenth century. Their sphere of influence was centered in northwestern and central Nigeria. Commercially powerful, the Hausa empire consisted of several centralized, walled, city-states that maintained persistent rivalries with one another and with the Kanem-Bornu empire to the northeast.

These two savanna kingdoms were eventually replaced by a third great empire that arose in the nineteenth century, the Fulani. These nomad pastoralists, led by Usman dan Fodio (1754–1817), waged war against the Hausa city-states in 1804 and conquered them by 1808. The Fulani then waged war on the Kanem-Bornu empire. The Kanem-Bornu empire eventually fell in 1846, with the execution of its last king. The Fulani rulers established a uniform system of government over a vast area and developed trading and commerce.

Kingdoms of the Southern Forests

In the dense forests of southwestern Nigeria, the Yorubas established a number of small, autonomous communities in about A.D. 1000. These settlements had large and elaborate castles in the center, surrounded by compounds for the artists and others who served the king. The Yorubas were prosperous traders who formed several kingdoms that flourished until the sixteenth century, when disputes among rulers led to their decline.

The kingdom of Benin was founded by the Edo people in the thirteenth century. Benin has little written history, but surviving terra-cotta sculptures and bronze castings indicate that the kingdom was culturally rich and economically active. Highly organized and backed by an efficient army, Benin controlled a large area northwest of the Niger Delta. The kingdom especially prospered between the fourteenth and seventeenth centuries.

Trade, particularly in slaves and horses, was a crucial factor in the rise of the kingdom of Benin. The kingdom became powerful in the seventeenth century partly due to horses that were used in cavalry forces. The horses came from the north and were unique in the south. Benin traded various goods, including ivory, pepper, and palm products, in return for horses and salt. Merchants also sold slaves to Europeans in return for cloth and other goods. This trade led to this part of the West African coast being called the "Slave Coast."

ANCIENT BENIN

The kingdom of Benin, one of western Africa's oldest civilizations, is famous for its ivory carvings and bronze sculptures (*above*).
(*A Closer Look, page 46*)

The Arrival of the Europeans

Until the late fifteenth century, Africa south of the Sahara had remained largely unknown to Europeans. The Portuguese were seeking trade and trade routes to Africa and Asia. They wanted to cut out the Arab traders, who had been acting as middlemen between Europe and the rest of the world. This quest for trade, as well as the desire to expand geographical knowledge, led Prince Henry of Portugal (1394–1460), better known as Henry the Navigator, to send expeditions to the western coast of Africa. In 1472, the Portuguese arrived in Benin.

The Portuguese began trading in gold, ivory, pepper, and, later, slaves. Trade was brisk and profitable for Africans and Portuguese alike. Portugal quickly recognized Benin as one of the most important kingdoms on the coast. The English, Dutch, and French soon arrived and joined the trade in slaves. By the seventeenth century, the slave trade was the most important trading activity on the western coast of Africa. By the end of the seventeenth century, Britain had overtaken Portugal as the largest slave-trading nation.

THE SLAVE TRADE

The Niger Delta was an important center of the slave trade from the late fifteenth to the early nineteenth centuries.
(A Closer Look, page 66)

Below: In the late nineteenth century, the British established trading posts along the Niger River, including this one in Asaba, southern Nigeria.

Explorers and Missionaries

In 1807, after years of political agitation over the issue, Britain's trade in slaves was abolished. Britain now sought new ways to trade with Africa and began to trade for palm oil and other agricultural products. The British also explored the Niger River in search of other natural resources.

In 1796, Mungo Park (1771–1806), a Scottish doctor, established that the Niger River flowed eastward, not westward as was previously thought. In 1823, explorers Dixon Denham (1786–1828) and Hugh Clapperton (1788–1827) reached the Hausa states and opened up trade with northern Nigeria via the Niger River. In 1830, Richard Lander (1804–1834) discovered that the Niger entered the South Atlantic Ocean through the Niger Delta.

With the opening up of the interior came missionaries and the spread of Christianity. These missionaries began to provide education and health care. In 1843, the Methodists established a post at Badagary. In 1846, the Church of Scotland started a school in Calabar, while the London Church Missionary Society opened its first station in Onitsha in 1857. The Roman Catholic Church soon followed, establishing its first church in Nigeria in 1885.

Above: **Scots Hugh Clapperton (*left*) and Mungo Park (*right*) explored northern Nigeria in the late eighteenth and early nineteenth centuries.**

Below: **British journalist Flora Shaw (1852–1929) was the first to suggest that Nigeria be named after the Niger River.**

Colonization

The importance of the trade on the Niger River led the European powers to divide West African territories among themselves. Britain was allotted the Niger Delta and the interior of the country. All of Nigeria soon came under British control, and in 1914, Nigeria became the Colony and Protectorate of Nigeria.

In the 1920s, however, Nigerians from different ethnic groups and backgrounds began asking for independence from Britain. In 1946, Britain began to take steps toward granting independence, and Nigeria gained independence on October 1, 1960.

Independence

Nigeria's first government after independence was headed by Prime Minister Sir Abubakar Tafawa Balewa (1912–1966). In 1963, Nigeria elected its first president, Nnamdi Azikiwe (1904–1996). The army came to power in 1966, however, and Nigeria was then run by a series of military governments, with only a short period of civilian rule between 1979 and 1983. The situation changed in May 1999, when Olusegun Obasanjo was declared president after elections held earlier that year. These elections marked Nigeria's return to democracy.

THE BIAFRAN WAR (1967–1970)

In 1967, the Igbos in the eastern part of Nigeria declared themselves independent and created their own state — Biafra. The federal government of Nigeria refused to recognize Biafra, and civil war ensued. The fighting lasted two and a half years, during which hundreds of thousands of Biafrans died from starvation and disease. The federal government finally defeated Biafran forces in January 1970.

Below: Nigerians in Lagos cheer as they celebrate independence from Britain on October 1, 1960.

Amina Sarauniya Zazzua (c.1533–c.1610)

Amina Sarauniya Zazzua was a princess born in Zazzua, an ancient Hausa city-state that existed near present-day Zaria in northern Nigeria. At the age of sixteen, she began learning how to rule her people. She also acquired military skills from her soldiers. She became queen of Zazzua in 1576 and began expanding Zazzua's territories. She ruled Zazzua for thirty-four years, during which time the city-state grew powerful.

Frederick John Lugard (1858–1945)

Born in India, Frederick John Lugard started his career as a soldier in the British army. He had served with distinction in Afghanistan, Sudan, and Myanmar before arriving in Africa. In northern Nigeria, he was responsible for the relatively peaceful establishment of British control in the late 1890s. His policy was to exercise control through the local rulers. In 1912, Lugard unified the administration of Nigeria's northern and southern regions. In 1914, he was appointed Nigeria's first governor general. He served for five years before retiring in 1919.

Frederick John Lugard

Nnamdi Azikiwe (1904–1996)

Nnamdi Azikiwe was Nigeria's first president. Born in northern Nigeria, he studied in the United States, where he distinguished himself as a bright and talented postgraduate student. In 1937, Azikiwe returned to Nigeria and entered the world of politics and publishing, producing books aimed at inspiring Nigerian nationalism.

He was the founder of a political party called the National Council of Nigeria and the Cameroons. His eloquence, personal charm, and commitment to Nigerian independence made him immensely popular with Nigerians.

Nnamdi Azikiwe

On November 16, 1960, Azikiwe was appointed Nigeria's first indigenous governor general; three years later, he became Nigeria's first post-independence president. He held this post until 1966, when he was removed from office by a military coup d'état. He attempted unsuccessfully to reenter politics in 1970 and, later, in 1983. Today, Nigerians recognize him as the father of Nigeria's independence.

Government and the Economy

Nigeria has a history of unstable governments. Since gaining independence from Britain in 1960, the country has suffered several military coups and failed attempts at democracy. A new democratic government, led by President Olusegun Obasanjo, was established in 1999. Nigerians are hopeful that the new government will improve the country's economy and reduce bribery and corruption.

Administration

Nigeria is a federal republic divided into thirty-six states and one territory administering the capital city, Abuja. The administration consists of the federal government, state governments, and local governments. The president, assisted by a vice-president and cabinet, heads the federal government. Each state is headed by a governor and House of Assembly. Local governments are run by elected councils. Each state controls its own health, education, transportation, and agricultural issues. Federal responsibilities include defense, foreign affairs, and internal security.

MAJOR CHALLENGES

The new democratic government in Nigeria faces many challenges, especially the fight against corruption. One of President Olusegun Obasanjo's first acts after being sworn into office in 1999 was to present an anticorruption bill to the National Assembly for enactment into law. Another problem is the religious tension that exists in many parts of the country. Pressing environmental issues include deforestation and air and water pollution.

TALE OF TWO CITIES

Lagos, Nigeria's largest city, was the country's capital until 1991. Overcrowded living conditions, a high crime rate, severe traffic congestion, and lack of room for expansion eventually convinced the Nigerian government to build a new, centralized capital city at Abuja.
(A Closer Look, page 68)

Left: Nigeria's Parliament House is one of Abuja's many imposing buildings.

Left: Government inspectors assess the quality of peanuts from sacks in Kano. Peanuts are grown mainly for export.

AGRICULTURE

About half of Nigeria's workers are farmers, and agriculture is a major part of the economy. However, Nigeria does not produce enough food for its growing population.
(A Closer Look, page 44)

The National Assembly is Nigeria's legislature and consists of the Senate and the House of Representatives. The president and members of the National Assembly are elected by the people to four-year terms. The federal government appoints judges to the Supreme Court, Nigeria's highest court. The country follows English common law, Islamic law, and tribal law.

Natural Resources and Industries

Nigeria is blessed with many natural resources. In addition to a large, industrious population, the country has large stores of mineral wealth, the most important of which is crude oil. Crude oil comes from the ground beneath the swamps of the Niger Delta and from offshore deposits in the Atlantic Ocean. Other resources include limestone, coal, iron ore, tin, columbite, and gold.

Agricultural products include cocoa, palm oil, and peanuts. Cocoa and palm produce are found in the forest belt in the south. Peanuts are grown in the savannas in the north. Other farm products are corn, rice, and yams. Farmers also raise goats, poultry, and sheep. The chief industrial products are cement, chemicals, fertilizers, food products, and textiles.

Below: The bright, reddish-orange fruit of the oil palm produces palm oil, one of Nigeria's exports.

Above: Workers on an oil rig near Bonny operate the machines that drill for oil.

Oil, Imports, and Exports

Nigeria's economy "floats" on oil, which accounts for 95 percent of the country's revenue. Oil was discovered in Nigeria in 1956, and commercial exploitation began in earnest after independence in 1960. Today, the country produces two million barrels of oil per day, making Nigeria the largest oil producer in Africa and the sixth biggest exporter in the world. Nigeria is an important member of OPEC, the Organization of Petroleum Exporting Countries. The oil is exported to many countries, including the United States, Canada, Britain, and South Africa.

Nigeria's economy is overly dependent on oil. The Nigerian government is trying to diversify the economy, reduce the nation's dependence on oil, and tackle the country's high foreign debt.

Nigeria's major trading partners are the United States and the European Union. Nigeria imports manufactured goods, machinery for oil production, transportation equipment, building materials, chemicals, and live animals. Nigerian exports, other than oil and petroleum products, include cocoa, rubber, and tin.

HIGH DEBTS

In the early 1970s, oil prices rose sharply, and the Nigerian government found itself with a huge surplus in revenue. As a result, the country approved large-scale development projects. By the 1980s, however, the price of oil had dropped, and Nigeria was forced to borrow heavily from other countries to pay for unfinished projects. Nigeria's foreign debts today are the highest in Africa.

Employment

Nigeria has a very high unemployment rate. The large cities have many small, informal businesses created by the unskilled workers in the country; for example, some workers park cars, others clean them, and others sell items to drivers stuck in traffic.

In 1999, 54 percent of the workforce was employed in the agricultural sector, 40 percent in the service sector, and 6 percent in the industrial sector.

Land, Sea, and Air Transportation

Most parts of Nigeria are connected by road and railway networks. Nigeria's highways and roads, however, suffer from poor maintenance and years of heavy freight traffic. The railway network, one of the first in Africa, has also been neglected, although steps are being taken to restore the system.

The major ocean ports in Nigeria are Lagos, Calabar, and Port Harcourt, while important inland river ports include Onitsha and Lokoja. Internal airplane flights connect major cities in Nigeria, with Kaduna, Enugu, and Port Harcourt having the busiest traffic. Three international airports — one each in Lagos, Abuja, and Kano — connect Nigeria to the rest of the world.

FISHING COMMUNITIES

The large number of rivers in Nigeria support a significant number of people who earn their living by fishing.
(A Closer Look, page 50)

Below: **As more and more Nigerians move from rural to urban areas, overcrowding and traffic jams are increasingly common in Lagos and other large cities.**

People and Lifestyle

Nigeria has the largest population in Africa. Latest estimates put the figure at around 123 million, making Nigeria home to one out of every five Africans. Nigerians have large families. Every year, new births alone equal the populations of some of the smaller African countries. The largest cities in Nigeria are Lagos, Ibadan, and Kano.

About 43 percent of Nigerians live in urban areas. Many of the features of city life, such as indoor plumbing and electricity, are not available in the countryside. Although a city of modern conveniences, Lagos has a high rate of crime, as well as serious problems of overcrowding and poverty.

Nigerians are dynamic, vivacious, hospitable, and friendly. They love to laugh and have a great sense of humor. They are also very fond of children. Outside the large cities, visitors are greeted with smiling and curious faces. In the large cities, particularly in a hot climate, tempers can fray quickly, but a joke can often calm a potentially difficult situation. Nigerians love giving and receiving gifts, which are called *dash* (DAHSH).

THE HAUSA-FULANI

The Hausa-Fulani (*above*) are the largest of Nigeria's ethnic groups. The group is called Hausa-Fulani because, since the nineteenth century, a large number of Fulani have become part of the Hausa group. The Hausa-Fulani peoples live in northern and central Nigeria and are famous as cattle herders. Some Fulani remain distinct from the Hausa and speak the Fulani language, Fulfulde.

Left: Young Wodaabe men in northern Nigeria wear bright clothes and make-up during a traditional male beauty contest.

Left: A Nigerian family and friends dance together at a birthday party in Ibadan.

THE YORUBA

The Yoruba have a rich history, culture, and artistic tradition. Historically, Yoruba land was divided into several states that used an ancient system of law. Their state capitals are now among the largest towns in the country. Yoruba believe they are descended from a common ancestor, *Oduduwa* (oh-doo-DOO-ah), who is said to have migrated from Arabia to the Nigerian town of Ife.

Ethnic Groups

Nigeria has more than 250 ethnic groups. The three main groups are the Hausa-Fulani in the north, the Yoruba in the southwest, and the Igbo, or Ibo, in the southeast. Together, these three groups make up more than two-thirds of Nigeria's population. Other ethnic groups include the Ijaw, Kanuri, Ibibio, Tiv, Edo, and Nupe peoples. Nigerians as a people have no common ancestry, and ethnic rivalries are fierce.

Family Life

As in most African countries, family ties are extremely important in Nigeria. The extended family includes uncles, aunts, and first, second, and third cousins, however many times removed. Family ties are more important than national or ethnic loyalties in moments of crisis. It is common, especially in eastern Nigeria, to hear a man talk of his brother when he is speaking of someone from the same village. Respect for elders is part of all Nigerian cultures, but it is especially important among the Yoruba.

THE IGBO

The Igbo, or Ibo, are known as an adventurous and industrious people. In the past, the Igbo lived in communal groups, which were autonomous and ruled by the elders of each clan. Today, many Igbo live in villages east of the Niger Delta, as well as in the bustling southern cities of Port Harcourt and Calabar. Many Igbo earn their living as professionals and civil servants.

Left: **Many women in Nigeria have carved out a role for themselves as traders and shopkeepers.**

The Role of Women

Women in Nigeria who live outside the traditional Muslim areas enjoy considerable freedom. Even in Muslim areas, where *purdah* (PURR-dah), or the complete veiling of a woman's face, is practiced, women still play an important role in the community, especially in commerce and trade. Nigerian women also hold positions of leadership in government.

Many Nigerian women have independent sources of income. Every village in Nigeria has its female traders. The education of women was not a priority in the past, but now education for girls is widespread. In the north, the Muslim culture did not equip women for modern roles, but the situation is slowly changing.

Some Muslim women are also subject to *kulle* (KEW-luh), or seclusion, within walled compounds. They accomplish a great deal, however, within the walls. For centuries, spinning cotton, frying bean cakes, and cooking millet dumplings for their children to sell in the neighborhood have provided these enterprising women with incomes.

COLORFUL TRADITIONAL CLOTHES

Nigerians are famous for their ethnic clothes (*above*). Textile arts have also had a long history in Nigeria. Dressing well is seen as showing respect to one's friends.

(A Closer Look, page 48)

Nigerian women have also gained an international reputation as leaders in academic and business circles. Many Nigerian women hold positions of responsibility in international organizations such as the World Bank and the International Monetary Fund.

National Youth Service Corps

Before entering the workforce, all university or college graduates must contribute national service in the Nigerian National Youth Service Corps. This involves military training for six weeks, followed by job placement in government, industry, or the private sector. Many graduates fulfill their national service duties by teaching in rural elementary and secondary schools.

Nigerian Names

Names are important in Nigeria, and they are usually short forms of a whole sentence. Naming ceremonies are held one week after a child's birth and are attended by family members and friends. Most names are religious in nature, with Islam and Christianity influencing the choice of names. Names in the north are mainly Islamic or Arabic in origin. In Christian areas, biblical and traditional African names are common.

Below: **Some Nigerian military officers join the armed forces after first serving in the National Youth Service Corps.**

Education

During British colonial times, Nigerian parents allowed only their weakest children to go to school, as these children were not strong enough to help with farm work. Today, Nigerian parents recognize the value of education; they know that education is the key to good jobs and wealth. Although about half the population has had no formal schooling, and only 57.1 percent of people aged fifteen and over are literate, Nigeria has produced scholars, experts, and professionals in many fields of learning.

Elementary School and Secondary School

Elementary school for most Nigerians usually begins at the age of six and continues to the age of eleven. Elementary school students study subjects ranging from mathematics and science to English and the three main Nigerian languages — Hausa, Yoruba, and Igbo. Some private schools offer computer studies and European languages. Students who successfully complete the Common Entrance Examination during their last year in elementary school obtain a school-leaving certificate and can then be admitted to secondary school.

Below: **Students in a private school in Lagos learn to play the recorder after regular class is over.**

Nigerian students spend six years in secondary school, or high school, until they are about seventeen years old. Secondary school is divided into two parts. Students spend the first three years preparing for the Junior Secondary School Examination. During the next three years, students study to pass two important examinations: the Ordinary Level exams and the Senior Secondary School Examination. Secondary school subjects include chemistry, economics, government, biology, and agriculture.

Above: **A student reads a poem during class at a school in Maiduguri, in Borno State.**

Higher Education

Nigerian society places great emphasis on higher education. Universities and polytechnics in Nigeria are run by the federal or state government and by private organizations. Students who wish to pursue higher education have a choice of thirty-seven universities and twenty-six polytechnic colleges.

Although polytechnic colleges were established to train students in technical skills, some of them now award degrees. In addition to awarding undergraduate degrees, some Nigerian universities award postgraduate master and doctoral degrees.

Above: **Muslim Nigerians gather for prayer on the grounds of a mosque in Kano.**

Religion

The main religions in Nigeria are Islam, Christianity, and traditional African religions. About 50 percent of the population is Muslim, while 40 percent is Christian; about 10 percent of Nigerians follow traditional African religions. Christianity is dominant in the south, and Islam in the north. Some southerners practice animism, or the belief that all natural objects possess a spirit. This belief is the basis of African traditional religions. Some Nigerians also combine Christian or Muslim beliefs and practices with traditional African beliefs.

Islam first reached northern Nigeria in the eleventh century via the trans-Saharan trade routes and subsequently spread across the country. Today, Islam affects all aspects of life in the north. Mosques are common, and the faith dictates the eating habits and dress of all believers. Like Muslims all over the world, Nigerian Muslims pray five times a day. Friday is the sacred day of prayer, and in large towns such as Kano, up to 50,000 people gather around the central mosque for prayer.

SHARI'A LAW

Some of Nigeria's northern states have adopted Islamic law, or *Shari'a* (SHAH-ree-yah) law. This law is based on the Qur'an and provides rules for Muslims. Not merely a legal code, Shari'a law includes rules for praying and fasting. Under Shari'a law, women are required to wear veils. Shari'a law also allows harsh physical punishment for crimes.

Christianity came to Nigeria later with the arrival of Catholic Portuguese traders in the late fifteenth century. Today, Catholics and Protestants are numerous, especially in southern Nigeria. A number of sects have combined Christianity with traditional beliefs. The Aladura (ah-lah-DOO-rah) Church is a unique result of the meeting between two distinct spiritual cultures: Christianity and traditional Yoruba religion. Other Christian groups include the charismatic and evangelical churches that were introduced from the United States. They are the fastest growing religious groups in Nigeria.

Several different variations of animism and African traditional beliefs exist. The shared principles are a belief in a supreme being who created all matter and in the spiritual nature of every object. For instance, flooding may be explained as the river god expressing his anger. Ancestor worship is also practiced. Followers offer animal sacrifices to appease deities, spirits, and ancestors. In the markets of southwestern Nigeria, vendors sell baskets of animal skulls, dried insects, bones, and different types of dried plants. These objects are commonly used in animistic ceremonies.

YORUBA RELIGION

Followers of traditional Yoruba religion, an animistic faith, believe in hundreds of deities, all of which are linked to the natural world. Yorubas also perform special rites to honor their ancestors.

(A Closer Look, page 72)

Below: **Christians pray at a church in Lagos.**

Language and Literature

Over 250 languages and dialects are spoken in Nigeria. English, however, is the official language and is used in government, commerce, and education. The three principal native languages are Yoruba in the southwest, Hausa in the north, and Igbo in southeastern Nigeria.

Pidgin English

English in Nigeria has been influenced by local languages. Colloquial pidgin English is a common form of spoken English. This variation of English is a mixture of standard English, mispronounced English, slang, and words from native languages.

Left: Using Arabic calligraphy, a young Hausa man in Zaria diligently copies pages from the Qur'an.

THE ARABIC LITERARY TRADITION

The history of Arabic writing in Nigeria is about eight hundred years old. The first writer known to use Arabic was Abu Ishaq Ibrahim al-Kanemi, a poet in Kano who lived in the thirteenth century. Kano, Katsina, and Ngazargamu emerged as centers of Arabic-Islamic learning in northern Nigeria. Other centers grew up in the nineteenth and twentieth centuries. Scholars of the Arabic literary tradition produced a huge amount of literature that covered many topics, from mathematics and theology to history and astronomy. Composing poems in Arabic was also a popular form of expression. Today, the use of Arabic as a literary and scholarly language in Nigeria remains strong, and many books are published in Arabic.

The Oral Heritage

Nigeria's oral traditions originated many centuries ago; culture and history have been passed down through an oral heritage. Nigerian oral literature includes performances, stories, proverbs, sayings, and songs. To this day, in many Nigerian communities, the practice of storytelling passes on cultural values, traditions, and codes of behavior.

Nigerian Literature

Nigeria has produced many gifted and award-winning writers, including Chinua Achebe, Wole Soyinka, Ben Okri, Amos Tutuola, and Cyprian Ekwensi. Outspoken and sometimes critical of their country's political Establishment, Nigerian writers address important issues in their works, such as poverty and justice.

Wole Soyinka is among the most versatile of Nigeria's writers. He has written over twenty plays, four volumes of poetry, and two novels. In 1986, Wole Soyinka won the Nobel Prize for Literature, only the fifth time that the prize had been awarded to a person from the developing world.

FLORA NWAPA

Another well-known writer is Flora Nwapa. An Igbo schoolteacher, she was the first Nigerian woman to publish a novel in English. Most of Nwapa's books are about the problems women face in marriage and society. Her books include *Efuru* (1966), *Idu* (1971), and *Wives at War and Other Stories* (1980).

Arts

African, and particularly Nigerian, art is recognized as some of the finest artwork in the world. Nigeria has an artistic tradition that stretches back over 2,000 years. The rich and varied art forms reflect the cultures and traditions of the numerous ethnic groups.

Nigerian art celebrates life, especially the respect for life and the unity of life and nature. Art forms include painting, sculpture, dance, drama, and wood carving. Nok sculptures are the earliest known form of Nigerian art. The most famous Nigerian art comes from the ancient kingdom of Benin. Archaeologists have unearthed beautiful examples of bronze, terra-cotta, and wooden sculptures representing human and mythical figures.

Nigeria's performing arts are particularly rich and include dance, drama, music, and drumming. Dancers are inspired by their rich cultural traditions. They also communicate the feelings and hopes of their audiences through music and movement. Dance performances often express emotions of love, joy, hope, sadness, and grief. Humor is an important part of Nigerian drama.

TRADITIONAL ARCHITECTURE

Nigerians use many materials to build their traditional dwellings. These materials include wood, earth, and brick.
(*A Closer Look, page 70*)

Below: These beautiful reliefs were carved into the city walls of Benin many centuries ago.

30

Above: **An Igbo wood-carver in Enugu works on a sculpture of an animal.**

Contemporary Visual Arts

Nigeria is famous not only for its ancient art, but also for its modern art. Jimoh Buraimoh, Ben Enwonwu, Twins Seven Seven, and Bruce Onobrakpeya are Nigerian artists who have gained international recognition for their contemporary artwork.

Buraimoh became well known in the 1960s for his bead pictures. He glues thousands of glass beads to wood, forming beautiful mosaics. His work can be seen hanging in many buildings around Nigeria and abroad. Onobrakpeya, an artist from the same generation, is internationally acclaimed for his use of various media, including plastic. He practices plastography, the art of molding figures out of plastic materials.

Musa Yola represents a new generation of Nigerian artists. He is a unique painter who literally paints the facades of houses and buildings, decorating them with checkerboard patterns, flower motifs, and human figures. Another artist, Mike Irrifere, has earned recognition for his paintings on board and paper. He paints human figures within their social settings.

Communal Arts

Communal art in Nigeria is art produced in local communities, usually by artists working in small groups. The crafts include wood carving, pottery, textile dyeing, weaving, and basketry. A great deal of the art appears on household articles, such as stools and bowls. Such art is both practical and decorative.

Certain regions are famous for specific crafts. Most regions have a cloth typically made in the area. Kano, in the north, is famous for beautiful indigo cloth. In the southwest, a type of woven cloth called *aso oke* (AH-so oh-kay) is a specialty, while *akwete* (ah-KWAY-tay) comes from southeastern Nigeria.

Calabash decoration is another distinctive Nigerian art. Calabashes are gourds that grow on calabash trees. Gourds range in size from those large enough to be used as rafts to those small enough for use as pepper pots. After the ripe fruit is scooped out of a gourd, the outer skin is dried. Once dried, designs are etched on the calabashes using knives and scrapers. Calabashes have practical uses. In the north, they are used to store milk. In other areas, calabashes are used as storage containers for grain.

Above: **Intricately designed carpets and mats are offered for sale in the Old Market in Kano. Many types of Nigerian textiles are considered works of art in their own right.**

Nigerian Music and Performing Arts

Music has always been an important part of Nigerian life. Native styles of music include the *agidigbo* (ah-GEE-DIG-boh), *kokoma* (koh-koh-MAH), and *juju* (JOO-joo). Sunny Ade and Fela Anikulapo Kuti are famous Nigerian singers.

Dance is an important part of Nigerian culture and serves as a form of both entertainment and religious ritual. Dance celebrations mark important stages in a person's life, including birth, initiations into adulthood, marriage, and death. Dance is also a form of healing in some Nigerian communities. The Tiv people of Nigeria have a dance that is said to combat disease and death. Some dances are a form of martial art, such as the *korokoro* (KOH-roh-KOH-roh) dance. During the *igbin* (IG-been) dance of the Yoruba, the order in which the dancers appear reflects their age and social status.

Drums are especially important in Nigerian dance, since they are the main rhythmic accompaniment that keep the dancers in step. Vigorous drumming accompanies the dance of the Urhobo women, who push their arms back and forth and contract their torsos in time with the accelerating drum beats.

Masquerades are another important art form in Nigeria. Igbo festivals are known for their colorful masquerade dancers, who wear elaborate, painted masks.

NIGERIAN RHYTHMS

Fela Kuti (*above*) was one of Nigeria's most famous singers in the 1970s. His son Femi Kuti has followed in his footsteps and is today one of Nigeria's greatest singing sensations.
(A Closer Look, page 54)

Left: **Traditional Hausa dancers and musicians perform at an outdoor concert in Lagos.**

Leisure and Festivals

At Home

Nigerians enjoy visiting one another's homes, and many middle-class Nigerians entertain their guests with home entertainment centers that include sound systems, televisions, and video recorders. Watching television is a popular pastime, and Nigerians have a choice of about forty television channels.

Many Yoruba people play *ayo* (AH-yo), an ancient African game played with seeds and a carved wooden board. The Igbos call this game *okwe* (OH-kway), and the Hausas *darra* (DAH-rah). Checkers and chess are also popular board games.

Markets

All over Africa, markets are social as well as shopping centers. People go to the markets to meet their friends, as well as to buy items. Markets are an important part of every settlement in Nigeria. Some markets are very famous, such as the fish markets

Below: **Nigerians gather at a roadside market in Ibadan.**

of Calabar and Lagos, as well as the Old Market in Kano. Nigerian markets are crowded, noisy, and colorful. People interact with one another, chatting and bargaining over fresh fruit, vegetables, spices, and live chickens, goats, and cows.

Sports

Soccer is the national sport of Nigeria, and most Nigerians participate as spectators. Nigerians also love other competitive sports, including basketball, field hockey, rugby, and volleyball. Tennis, squash, golf, and polo are also popular, but these sports are played mostly by wealthy people. Most towns have a public stadium or sports field for soccer, track and field events, jogging, and aerobics. Sports are an important part of the school curriculum, and being a successful sportsperson is prestigious.

People from all walks of life play table tennis, or Ping-Pong, and billiards. Tables for these games are often set up on street corners. The tables are makeshift, made of simple materials such as wood, pieces of cardboard, and cloth.

PASSION FOR SOCCER

Nigeria's national sport is soccer. Many Nigerian soccer players are well known and play for top teams in the United Kingdom, France, Italy, and Germany.

(A Closer Look, page 58)

35

Left: Nigerian boxer Olusegun Ajose (*left*) gets close to his opponent during a boxing match at the 2000 Olympic Games in Sydney, Australia.

Nigerian International Sports Stars

Nigerian athletes are well known on the international stage, especially in track and field, boxing, and soccer. Some Nigerian soccer players play for top soccer teams in the United Kingdom. They include Nwankwo Kanu and Celestine Babayaro, who play for Arsenal and Chelsea soccer clubs, respectively.

The Nigerian national soccer team, the Super Eagles, has performed well internationally. The team has won gold and silver medals several times in the Africa Cup of Nations competition. The team also qualified for the World Cup in 1994 and won the gold medal in soccer at the 1996 Olympic Games. The Super Eagles advanced to the second round in the 1998 World Cup and the quarter final round in the 2000 Olympics. The women's team, the Super Falcons, is also gaining recognition, with good performances at the Olympic Games and World Cup.

Nigerian boxers have also made a name for themselves, with encouraging performances at the Olympic Games. Famous boxers include Jegbefumere Albert and David Izonritei.

Nigeria's men's 1,600-meter relay team won a silver medal at the 2000 Olympic Games in Sydney, while hurdler Glory Alozie won an individual silver medal. Women's weightlifter Ruth Ogbeifo won Nigeria's third Olympic silver medal in Sydney.

Above: Nwankwo Kanu is a famous Nigerian soccer player who plays for Arsenal Football Club, a soccer team in the United Kingdom.

Festivals

Nigerians celebrate many festivals each year. These celebrations commemorate public occasions, including religious holidays and historical events, as well as private occasions, such as births and initiations into adulthood.

Id al-Fitri Celebrations

Id al-Fitri (EED ahl-FIT-ree) celebrates the end of the Islamic fasting month of Ramadan, and Muslims throughout the country celebrate with feasting and praying.

The most colorful celebrations take place in northern Nigeria, where parades are part of the festivities. Hausa-Fulani horsemen wear breastplates, coats of flexible armor, and scarlet turbans topped with feathers. Their horses are also ornately decorated. The emir, or traditional leader, wears white robes and is protected from the sun by a white umbrella. After the emir takes his seat in a large square in front of his palace, various groups of horsemen charge toward him, halting just before the throne. The horsemen then salute the emir. This is called the *sallah* (SAH-lah) ceremony.

Below: **Horsemen wearing regal and elaborate costumes take part in a cavalry procession during Id al-Fitri celebrations in Kano.**

Argungu Fishing Festival

In mid to late February, the famous Argungu Fishing Festival takes place on the banks of the Sokoto River in Argungu, southwest of Sokoto. This three-day festival attracts visitors from all over the world.

Several months before the festival, the river is dammed, and all fishing is prohibited. Once the festival begins, however, literally hundreds of fishermen, some as young as ten years old, jump into the river with their nets and gourds. The scene is quite spectacular as they splash in the water, hoping to catch the biggest fish of the festival with their bare hands, nets, or calabashes. Some fishermen net fish weighing over 110 pounds (50 kilograms).

Pategi Regatta

The Pategi Regatta takes place around August on the Niger River, halfway between the towns of Ibadan and Kaduna. The regatta is one of the most photographed festivals in Nigeria. Events include fishing, swimming competitions, traditional dancing, and acrobatic displays. The highlight of the festival is the boat racing.

Below: **Fishermen use nets, calabashes, and their bare hands to catch fish during the Argungu Fishing Festival, which is held on the Sokoto River.**

National Day

October 1 is Nigeria's National Day. This public holiday celebrates Nigeria's independence from Britain in 1960. Military troops parade in the streets during the day, while public lectures and local film premiers mark festivities in the evening.

Above: **Young people wait to enter the colorful, inflated play areas called "bouncy castles" that have been set up at a children's festival in Lagos.**

Other Festivals

The Oshun Festival , held in August in Oshogbo, honors *Oshun* (oh-SHOON), the Yoruban river goddess of abundance and fertility. Dance dramas and traditional offerings are part of the ceremonies that take place to honor Oshun

Ikeji (ee-KAY-jee) is a festival of music and dance celebrated by certain Igbo clans. Colorfully dressed and masked dancers keep audiences enthralled with their elaborate costumes.

The *Igue* (ee-GOO-ay) Festival in Benin City is believed to be one of the oldest celebrations in Nigeria. It is celebrated to mark the end of the year in Benin and the start of the new year. This colorful festival featuring the best of Benin life and culture attracts many tourists from around the world.

Food

Food is an important part of Nigerian culture. Each part of the country has its special delicacies, but certain foods are eaten by everyone. The staples are tapioca, millet, corn, yams, rice, beans, and plantains, which are large, starchy bananas that must be cooked before eating. Chili peppers and spices, such as garlic, ginger, pepper cloves, and mixed herbs, are essential in Nigerian cooking.

Pastes and Soups

All of the staple foods can be pounded into flour, mixed with water, and cooked as a paste. Tapioca, for instance, is made into *eba* (EE-bah), and corn, millet, and rice are made into *tuwo* (TOO-woh). Yams can be eaten boiled, fried, or pounded into the Yoruba delicacy, pounded yam. Pastes are eaten with thick, rich soups.

Egusi (ee-GOO-see) soup is a favorite dish made with meat or fish, red peppers, onions, dried shrimp, crushed melon seeds,

Below: **An extended family gathers in the courtyard to help prepare a traditional Nigerian meal.**

Left: **Puff-puffs are local doughnuts that are sold as street snacks in Nigeria.**

and spinach. Okra soup is made in the same way but uses okra instead of melon seeds and spinach. Other soups are bitter leaf soup, peanut soup, and pepper soup, which is hot and very spicy. Pastes and soups are eaten with the hands. Little balls of the paste are formed between the fingers of the right hand. These balls are then dipped into the soup before eating.

Nigerian cuisine includes many rice dishes. Rice is boiled with meat, fish, or chicken in stews. One of the most famous Nigerian dishes is *jollof* (JAW-lof) rice, which is rice cooked with tomatoes and meat. Other types of rice preparation include coconut rice and fried rice. Nigerians also eat several types of beans, but the black-eyed variety is the most common. They can be eaten plain, but they are often made into a tasty, steamed cake called *moyin-moyin* (MOH-yeen-MOH-yeen).

Street Snacks

Several different kinds of snack foods are prepared in the street by roadside vendors. These snacks include fried yam chips and roasted peanuts. Other savory snack foods are *akara* (ah-KAH-rah), a fried snack made from beans, and *kulikuli* (KOO-lee-KOO-lee), a small ball of peanut paste. Sweet snacks include *chin-chin*, or fried pastry strips, and *puff-puff*, a local doughnut. *Suya* (SOO-yah) a hot, spicy piece of meat grilled on a stick, is also popular.

Below: **A man in Jos sells suya by the side of the road. Suya is a hot, spicy piece of meat grilled on a stick.**

41

A CLOSER LOOK AT NIGERIA

Since independence, Nigeria has often been associated in the foreign media with military dictatorships and the human suffering of the Biafran War (1967–1970). The Nigerian government also received much criticism over the execution of Nigerian author and activist Ken Saro-Wiwa and the "Ogoni Eight," who were perceived as having fought for human rights. Although rich in resources, Nigeria has had a history of military leaders who mismanaged the economy, neglected endangered wildlife, and failed to protect the country from pollution.

Below: **Hausa women wearing colorful skirts take a walk in Kaduna.**

Despite Nigeria's troubled political history, the country has many positive aspects, such as its exceptional cultural and artistic heritage. Nigerian athletes have won many international sports events and are known around the world. Nigerian musicians, including Sunny Ade and Fela Kuti, have made Nigerian music well known in many countries.

The people of Nigeria are friendly and hardworking. They are particularly proud of their heritage. Although composed of over 250 ethnic groups, Nigeria has maintained its unity while celebrating the colorful diversity of its many peoples.

Opposite: **A boat floats down the Niger River near Onitsha.**

Agriculture

Nigeria once grew enough crops to feed its people and even produced surpluses, which were exported. The agricultural sector, however, has not been able to keep up with the population growth. Today, Nigeria is unable to grow enough crops to feed its growing population and, therefore, has to import food.

Challenges

Natural disasters also have contributed to Nigeria's food shortages. The periodic droughts in the Sahel region reduce harvests and kill cattle. In the north, locusts sometimes wipe out an entire season's crops. Palm oil production in the southeast is still recovering from the effects of the Biafran War.

As more and more people work in the cities, fewer people take up farming as a livelihood. Even so, the agricultural sector in Nigeria still employs about 54 percent of the workforce. Yields are often poor, since most farm work is done by hand. Machinery, fertilizers, and pesticides are often too expensive for farmers.

Many city-dwelling Nigerians can now afford to eat more expensive foods. This situation has led to an increase in imports

CROPS

Nigeria produces a variety of crops including cocoa, cotton, and groundnuts. Cocoa and cotton are cultivated mostly in the forest belt of southern Nigeria. Groundnuts are grown in the savannas of the north. Other farm products are beans, cassava, corn, millet, rice, and yams.

Below: Nigerian farmers in Zamfara State plow the land with traditional iron and wooden tools.

of non-indigenous food products, with a resulting decrease in demand for similar local produce. Although Nigeria has significant fishing resources, for example, the country is the world's largest market for stockfish from Scandinavia.

Above: **Large sacks of onions wait to be sealed in the Old Market in Kano.**

Agricultural Incentives

The Nigerian government realizes the importance of producing sufficient food for the population. In the 1970s, "Operation Feed the Nation" was launched. The objective of this huge campaign was to make farming popular. During that time, large quantities of fertilizer were distributed free of charge, and a fund was set up to guarantee loans to farmers. In the 1980s, large-scale farming techniques that increased crop yields were introduced. The aim was to improve the agricultural sector and reduce food shortages.

Agriculture is a priority of the current government, which provides funds for irrigation systems, electricity, storage facilities, and new technology. The government continues to encourage rural investment by providing incentives for farmers and investors. Although agricultural production has increased, these programs have not solved the country's food problems.

Ancient Benin

Ancient Benin in the southwestern part of Nigeria was a particularly powerful kingdom in West Africa. Historians believe the kingdom developed in the twelfth century and remained a significant power through the seventeenth century. Although the kingdom ceased to exist when the British annexed it in 1897, the cultural and religious aspects of Benin survive to this day. The *oba* (OH-bah), or ruler, of Benin maintains a ceremonial role in the colorful festivals of present-day Benin City.

The Oba of Benin

In the past, the oba of Benin was believed to be descended from gods. He was worshiped by his subjects, and his public appearances were accompanied by great pomp and ceremony. Ordinary people approached the oba with great reverence, always from a distance, and on their knees. The oba would never allow himself to be seen eating, so the people believed he lived without food. The title of oba was hereditary, and he had total control over the people once he took office.

Above: **The Benin empire was famous for its works of art, including beautiful bronze sculptures of animals.**

Left: **Edo men dressed in traditional clothes await the arrival of the oba of Benin City.**

Benin's Religion

The people of Benin worshiped a variety of gods, including a supreme god, *Osanobua* (oh-san-oh-BOO-ah), who created the world. Every citizen had a personal god called an *ehi* (AY-hee). A person's ehi was his or her spiritual guide and link to Osanobua. The gods were honored with offerings at elaborate altars. Offerings included cowrie shells, coconuts, yams, and palm oil.

Above: **A musician from Benin City plays a traditional silver pipe.**

Art and Architecture

The capital of the empire, Benin City, was defended by a wall and a deep moat, both of which encircled the city. Parts of the wall and the moat are still visible today. The city had many tall towers on which enormous brass sculptures of birds perched.

The most famous Benin artifacts are bronze sculptures and plaques, some dating back to the thirteenth century. Bronze making was an art to glorify the oba. Artisans were also known for their ivory and wood carvings. They created superbly carved ornaments, bells, doors, and pillars, many of which are now displayed in museums throughout the world. Today, traditional methods of making bronze sculptures continue in Benin City.

Colorful Traditional Clothes

Nigerian traditional dress is worn along with Western dress for work, rest, and play. Textiles have always been valuable to Nigerians and symbolize culture. Today, a variety of different fabrics and garments are sold in shops and markets, from locally dyed cloth and cloth woven on traditional looms to Swiss lace and imported cotton. Rich, bold colors are popular.

Some types of clothing are worn by all Nigerians, regardless of ethnic backgrounds. Other clothes and styles of dress indicate the region from which people come as well as their ethnic backgrounds. Women often wear long skirts and tops made of printed fabrics called "up and down." Also popular is the *boubou* (BOO-boo), which is a comfortable, flowing robe with open sides. Many men wear loose, tapered trousers called *sokoto* (so-KOH-toe) and a tunic called a *buba* (BOO-bah).

Left: Children wear traditional Nigerian clothes at a Lagos fair.

The North

Hausa dress is popular throughout Nigeria and other parts of West Africa. The men wear long white robes. Little white, hand-woven caps are worn with this type of dress. The women, like many women elsewhere in Nigeria, wear simple blouses and long lengths of cloth wrapped around their hips.

The Southwest

The *agbada* (ahg-BAH-dah) is the everyday wear of Yoruba men. It is a gown worn over the buba and sokoto. Made of lace and cotton, the agbada is a loose, flowing garment with elaborate patterns on the front. The *dansiki* (dahn-SEE-kee) is a loose tunic matched with loose trousers. On festive occasions, women wear two pieces of brightly colored aso oke cloth. One is tied as a turban, while the other is draped over the shoulder or tied around the hips.

Below: This woman in Onitsha wears clothes of intricate patterns made from traditional methods of dyeing.

The Southeast

In the southeast, Igbo clothing of both men and women features the *lappa* (LAH-pah), a cloth wound around the waist and twisted and tucked in the front for men and at the back or side for women. Some men wear a shirt with shirttails hanging outside the lappa. Women wear the lappa with lace blouses and turbans.

Fishing Communities

The fishing industry is an important part of the economy of most Nigerian states. Both offshore sea and inland river fishing provide a great variety of fish and shellfish. Fishing communities thrive along the Nigerian coast and on riverbanks throughout the country. Most fish found in Nigerian waters are edible.

The River People

Lagos is a large commercial and harbor city straddling three islands and the mainland. Fishing communities line the shores. Homes in these fishing communities are built on stilts in the shallow water close to land. Houses are made of timber with corrugated iron roofs, and the houses are connected by a series of rough, wooden planks.

Conditions are difficult for people in the fishing communities. No adequate sanitary facilities exist, and electricity is also not sufficient to meet the needs of the residents.

FISHING METHODS

Some fisherfolk cast nets from dugout canoes to catch fish in the creeks around the islands of Lagos. Others fish from canoes with calico sails in the deeper waters of the Lagos lagoon. Still others set fish traps in the shallow waters near the mainland.

Below: **An Ijaw father and son dry their nets near Bonny.**

Fishing in the Delta

Nigerians have been fishing in the waters of the Niger Delta for centuries. Using wooden dugout canoes and paddles, they cast their nets into the surrounding sea and inland creeks. The actual fishing is usually done by men, but women are also involved in fishing activities; women stay behind in the villages to dry the fish for sale at markets.

Today, the delta is so polluted that weeks of fishing in the open sea may produce very poor yields. Sometimes all the fishermen catch are small fish. These fish, which normally would be thrown back into the sea, are now brought home for the family to eat. In the past, fisherfolk were respected and honored; today, however, they are poor and lead very hard lives.

The Northern Wetlands

The Nguru Wetlands in the north are also home to small fishing communities. The main pieces of fishing equipment used in Nguru are nets and gourds. The gourds act as floats and containers, while the nets are used to catch fish. Canoes are rarely used. The fishermen wade into lake or river waters to fish. The communities tend to have both farmers and fisherfolk.

The "Lost" Tribe of Koma

In 1987, the Koma tribe was "discovered" in Adamawa State, living in the Loh Mountains close to the border with Cameroon.

According to their history, the Koma were forced to flee into the mountains during Usman dan Fodio's religious wars in the early nineteenth century. They then lived in a world of their own until the 1930s, when they came into contact with Christian missionaries. The missionaries introduced health care and education, but serious attempts at helping the Koma began only after their "discovery" by a television company in 1987.

Following all the media attention on the Koma tribe, the government launched large-scale projects to help integrate the Koma into Nigerian society. A committee was formed to look into the needs of the Koma people. The Koma were resettled at the base of the mountains, where they live today. The government also dug water wells and built roads to allow access to Koma villages.

Left: **The Koma live at the base of the remote mountains of eastern Nigeria, close to the border with Cameroon.**

The Koma Today

Efforts to integrate the Koma into Nigerian society have been only partly successful. The Koma continue to live isolated lives in mud huts at the base of the mountains. Few of them have heard of Abuja or the head of state. Most of the Koma have never seen a car, and the sound of a car engine frightens them. In spite of being so isolated, the Koma people are open and friendly to strangers.

The Koma worship a god they believe brings peace and protection. They tell the time by judging the position of the sun in the sky. Many of the Koma wear animal skins, but some have trousers and T-shirts, which they have bought with grain at the local market of a nearby village. The market is one day's walk from the Koma villages, and only designated Koma people take produce to the market.

Koma women are shy and sit away from the men. They wear animal skins and skirts made from leaves. Both men and women carry babies on their backs in goatskin slings. Women must have their front teeth extracted before they get married. Otherwise, they believe they will be infertile.

Islam is unknown, but Christian missions are active. Schools and clinics have been built in this area. Medical facilities are dealing with the frequent outbreaks of diseases, such as measles and small pox, that the Koma have never been exposed to before.

Nigerian Rhythms

Music in the Ancient Past

Music has a long history in Nigeria and the rest of western Africa. Images of musical instruments are depicted on ancient stone and terra-cotta artifacts from Ife. Two of the instruments represented on the artifacts are the cylindrical igbin drum and the hourglass-shaped *dundun* (DOON-doon) drum. They were traditionally played by skilled drummers in praise of a king or a deity. Dundun drums are still used in traditional Yoruba festivals and rituals today. The bronze plaques of Benin also show horns, bells, and lutes. These historical records demonstrate the importance of music in ancient Nigeria.

Music of the Colonial Era

The music of the colonial period was dominated by European ballroom dance music, as well as jive, samba, and calypso music, which were musical styles developed by Africans in the Americas.

Below: **Drummers at the Offala festival in Oshogbo play the dundun drums.**

Popular indigenous music included juju music, with its lyrics dealing with local life, and highlife music, played by drum and brass bands. One of the most famous Nigerian musicians of 1940s and 1950s was Ernest Tunde Thomas. He was more popularly known as "Tunde, the Western Nightingale."

Above: **Femi Kuti, son of Fela Kuti, performs at Glastonbury in the United Kingdom.**

Fela Kuti

In the 1970s, Fela Anikulapo Kuti introduced Afro-beat to Nigeria. Afro-beat is a mixture of African rhythms and American soul music. Kuti's music was socially and politically motivated. His songs encouraged people to stand up for their rights. He was one of Nigeria's most famous singers and was very popular in Africa. He was imprisoned several times because some of his lyrics protested against Nigeria's military governments. Kuti died on August 2, 1997.

Below: **Sunny Ade is one of Nigeria's most beloved musicians.**

Modern Music

Nigerians appreciate a variety of musical styles, including the juju, highlife, and Afro-beat. American music, particularly hip-hop, rap, and jazz, has attracted many Nigerian fans. Christianity has also influenced popular music, and gospel music is heard everywhere.

Nok Culture

In 1928, tin miners digging on the Jos Plateau accidentally stumbled upon terra-cotta figurines. These figurines of human heads revealed an ancient culture, which archaeologists subsequently named Nok, after the town in which the first terra-cotta was discovered. Nok culture is recognized as the earliest organized civilization in Nigeria. This civilization flourished between 500 B.C. and A.D. 200.

The Terra-Cottas

The terra-cotta, or fired clay, sculptures range in size from small pendants to life-size figures. They are mainly human heads and effigies, but animals, especially snakes, are also represented.

Nok art has certain distinctive traits. The heads have pronounced mouths and eyes. The lower part of the eye is a triangle or half circle. The pupils of the eye are round holes, as are the ears, nostrils, and mouth. Most of the heads are cylindrical, but some are conical or spherical in shape. The sculptures have elaborate hairstyles in a shell or braid pattern. Some of the sculptures have headdresses or are decorated with pearl jewelry.

WHERE TO SEE NOK FIGURINES

Nok figurines are exhibited in Nigerian museums, as well as in museums overseas. Nok sculptures are in great demand by European and American art collectors. This demand has led to the looting of sculptures from archaeological sites, causing permanent damage and loss of valuable information.

Below: Terra-cotta pottery of various kinds is available to tourists who visit the Jos area.

56

The terra-cottas show that the Nok people probably raised crops and cattle. Both men and women enjoyed personal adornment, especially of the hair. Evidence suggests that Nok art and culture spread over a wide area. Traces of Nok culture are still identifiable in the daily lives of central and southern Nigerians.

Above: **Beautiful and distinctive Nok sculptures are on display at the National Museum in Lagos.**

Stone Age to Iron Age

The terra-cottas reveal that Nok culture was initially a Late Stone Age culture. In time, the Nok people discovered iron technology. They discovered that by heating certain rocks, they were able to melt the ore and obtain the refined iron. Easily molded, the iron then could be reshaped into weapons, plows, and cooking utensils.

Most ancient cultures passed through stages of discovering copper and bronze before iron, but the Nok seem to have entered the Iron Age directly from the Stone Age. Did the Nok discover iron technology by themselves, or did they learn its secrets from another culture? This fact remains a mystery to archaeologists.

Passion for Soccer

A Sport for All

Nigerians are passionate about soccer. Called football in Nigeria, soccer is the country's national sport and is played everywhere, from soccer fields to street corners and open spaces in villages. The sport is enjoyed by young and old alike and by people of all socioeconomic groups. Soccer is also the most popular spectator sport. Some say soccer is the only thing that unites Nigerians.

Organized Football

Organized football began in Nigeria in 1945, with the formation of the Nigerian Football Association. In 1959, Nigeria became a member of the Fédération Internationale de Football Association (FIFA), the world body that governs soccer. Nigeria now has dozens of football clubs in its national professional league.

The main national team is called the Super Eagles. The under-21 team is called the Flying Eagles, and the under-17 team, the

Below: **Celestine Babayaro (***left***) plays for Chelsea Football Club in the United Kingdom. During the 2000 Olympic Games in Sydney, he was captain of Nigeria's soccer team, which included Azubuike Oliseh (***right***).**

Golden Eaglets. These names reflect Nigeria's national symbol, the eagle.

Above: **Nwankwo Kanu (*second from left*) kicks the ball past his opponents during a league match in the United Kingdom.**

International Players

Nigerian football began to gain prominence internationally in 1980, when the Super Eagles won the African Cup of Nations. A Dutch coach, Clemence Westerhoff, played an important role in the development of Nigerian soccer by grooming several players in the junior league. Westerhoff then helped some of the players join top teams in Europe. These players included Stephen Keshi and Rashidi Yekini. They played very well, and their success has led to a steady flow of Nigerian players to European teams.

Currently, Nigeria has several well-known players in major leagues around the world. Nwankwo Kanu plays for Arsenal Football Club and Celestine Babayaro plays for Chelsea Football Club, both in the United Kingdom. Sunday Oliseh plays for the German team Borussia Dortmund, while Jay-Jay Okocha plays for Paris St. Germain in France. Taribo West plays for the English soccer team Derby County.

WOMEN'S SOCCER

Women's soccer, though not as popular as men's, is gaining recognition. The women's national team, the Super Falcons, participated in the women's World Cup in the United States in 1999 and at the 2000 Olympics in Sydney. Although they did not win a medal, several players won scholarships to play in the United States and are doing very well.

Pollution in the Delta

The Niger Delta has been producing oil since the 1950s and, today, produces about two million barrels of crude oil per day. Ninety percent of Nigeria's wealth comes from this oil. The delta, however, remains poor and undeveloped. Many regions of the delta have no clean drinking water, hospitals, schools, roads, or telecommunications. In addition, the delta suffers from environmental problems caused by the oil industry.

Above: **Nigeria is one of the main producers of petroleum in Africa.**

Challenges Facing the People of the Delta

Oil spills have destroyed fishing areas and farmlands. They have also polluted wells and beaches. People complain of suffering from skin disorders thought to be from oil-related contamination. These problems have devastated the health and livelihood of the people of the region, most of whom are fishermen and farmers.

Another problem is caused by gas flares. A lot of gas comes to the surface during the extraction of crude oil. The excess gas is burned off through pipes coming out of the ground. The gas flares burn continuously in several areas of the delta. These areas are always bright and hot; because of the heat and smoke, little vegetation grows. The flares affect fishing areas; the heat moves the fish away and affects their mating patterns. The smoke from the flares may also cause breathing disorders in humans.

What Has Caused the Problems?

Nigeria's revenue is controlled from Abuja. Revenue generated from all parts of the country goes into federal reserves, from which it is distributed. Revenues from oil are used to solve problems in other states, leaving little money for the Niger Delta.

The government and the oil companies have long neglected environmental issues. Nigeria has regulations to protect the environment, but the government has difficulty enforcing these laws. The enforcement agencies do not have enough trained personnel or the political power to control the pollution.

Nigeria's Ministry of the Environment has overall responsibility for the environment. In addition, each state has a State Ministry of the Environment, which oversees environmental issues at state level. Grass-roots groups also address environmental

DANGERS TO LIFE

Wildlife in the Niger Delta is badly affected by the oil industry. Animals are killed directly by the pollution or indirectly when their food source dies from pollution. In some areas, for example, red algae grows in abundance because the organisms that feed on it have been killed by pollution. The overgrowth of red algae in turn prevents oxygen from reaching riverbeds and suffocates organisms living at the bottoms of rivers.

issues. Private oil companies and the Nigerian National Petroleum Corporation, however, are more powerful than the ministries, making it difficult for ministries to enforce environmental laws.

Grass-Roots Activism

The number of delta-based community interest groups demanding a share in oil revenues has grown. The issue has become a heated one and has resulted in community unrest and ethnic conflict. Cases of oil workers being taken hostage and oil rigs being hijacked are not uncommon.

Nigeria's return to democracy has increased the expectations of the people of the Niger Delta. They want to see an improvement in their living standards. The new government appears to be committed to accelerating economic development in the area. In 2000, the administration took steps to tackle the problems by passing the Niger Delta Development Commission Act. This law proposes a new framework for the development of the Niger Delta. With this law, the problems of the delta may yet be solved.

KEN SARO-WIWA

Ken Saro-Wiwa was an Ogoni activist. The Ogoni live in one of the oil-producing areas of the delta that is polluted by the oil industry. Saro-Wiwa formed the National Youth Council of Ogoni People to fight for fairer distribution of oil revenues. Saro-Wiwa and eight others were blamed for causing the deaths of some Ogoni chiefs and were executed in 1995 by the military government.

Below: Oil refineries in the Niger Delta are often built close to towns and villages. This refinery is in Rivers State.

Precious Forests

Deforestation is a major problem in Nigeria, and primary forests have nearly vanished. Conservation efforts in the Omo Forest Reserve, however, have been relatively successful, and the forest continues to thrive.

The reserve is located in the state of Ogun, about two hours from Lagos. The forest is one of the few remaining tropical rain forests in Nigeria and is home to many species of plants and animals, including some that are endangered.

The reserve occupies an area of 1,150 acres (465 hectares) and supports many animals, including the forest elephant, antelope, and warthog. The reserve also supports many species of birds.

The reserve is divided into two parts: a central zone and an outer zone encircling it. The central zone is largely undisturbed. The area used to be heavily exploited by hunters and farmers, but

Left: **Some of Nigeria's last remaining tropical rain forests grow in Ogun State.**

now plants and animal populations are recovering. Other rain forests in Nigeria include those in Cross River and Oyo states.

Above: **Nigeria's few remaining forests support many animals, including monkeys, elephants, antelope, and a diverse population of bird species.**

Conservation Efforts

Many measures are in place to help ensure the survival of Omo's forests. Controlling hunting is one of them. To better understand hunting patterns, price surveys of wild-animal meat sold at local markets are carried out. Local village families are also educated about other sources of protein. Fishing in the rivers of the forest, snail farming, and beekeeping have been introduced. Some revenue is obtained from tourism, as visitors are allowed into the outer areas of the reserve.

Threats to Nigeria's Forests

Nigeria's conservationists are urging the government to take away concessions that were awarded to timber companies and to tighten national laws on logging. Pressure is also on the government to introduce a logging charter. Lax laws regarding land use have led to the loss of over 90 percent of Nigeria's forests in just forty years. Forest reserves that are under threat include not only the Omo forests, but also reserves in Cross River State and other parts of southern Nigeria.

Saving the Lowland Gorilla

In 1987, a survey established the presence of gorillas in pockets of forest in southeastern Nigeria, along the border with Cameroon. The find was significant, since gorillas previously were thought to be extinct in Nigeria. Two types of gorillas live in Nigeria. The Mbe Mountains and Afi River Forest Reserve are home to the western lowland gorillas (*Gorilla gorilla gorilla*), while the gorillas of Cross River National Park are classified as the Cross River gorillas (*Gorilla gorilla diehli*). Both species of lowland gorillas are endangered.

Numbers and Habitat

The gorillas of the Mbe Mountains and Afi River Forest Reserve live in small patches of forest scattered across rugged hill country. At about one hundred gorillas, the total size of these populations is very small. Their habitat continues to shrink as a result of deforestation. Only about twenty gorillas inhabit the Cross River National Park. They live in lowland forests and river valleys.

Below: **A lowland gorilla plays with her infant in the Afi River Forest Reserve.**

Threats to the Survival of Nigeria's Gorillas

Hunting is the main cause of the shrinking gorilla populations. Gorillas are hunted not only as big game trophies by illegal poachers, but also for meat. Locals also believe that gorilla hands and feet have medicinal properties. A number of gorillas, especially infants, are captured for sale abroad. The mothers are killed, and the infants are taken alive. An estimated fifteen gorillas are killed each year, but only ten babies are born in that time. Nigeria's gorillas will be extinct very soon if hunting is not properly controlled.

The large-scale clearing of the forest has reduced the gorillas' habitat. Gorillas in the Mbe Mountains are being pushed higher and higher into the mountains. This destruction of the natural environment breaks up gorilla communities and keeps them isolated not only from each other but also from potential conservation efforts.

Above: **A lowland gorilla cradles her dead infant in the Sydney Zoo. The baby gorilla died a few days after being born. The grieving mother did not release the body until a few days later. The baby was the first naturally born lowland gorilla in an Australian zoo.**

Efforts at Conservation

Gorillas are protected by law in Nigeria, but enforcement of the law is poor. The government has tried to control the hunting of gorillas by establishing reserves and employing game wardens, but these methods have been only partially successful. Poachers continue to defy and escape the authorities. The game wardens occasionally find their own lives threatened when they defend the gorillas from aggressive hunters.

The Nigerian Conservation Foundation and other environmental bodies are working with the government to protect the gorillas. These organizations have negotiated with villagers in the reserves to stop hunting gorillas and have tried to provide alternative sources of income for the villagers. The conservationists' aim is to establish areas in the reserves where hunting is completely banned.

The government is also trying to encourage ecotourism in order to provide another means of income for the locals. Ecotourism is the practice of touring natural habitats with minimum damage to the environment. In this way, locals can earn a living as park guides. The Obudu Cattle Ranch in the Cross River National Park already has a tourist center and lodge. The ranch is being renovated and is planning tours that will allow visitors to view the gorillas in their natural surroundings.

The Slave Trade

Slavery was a long-standing custom in Africa. The practice increased in scale, however, with the arrival of Arab Muslims and Europeans. The Atlantic slave trade developed after the Portuguese established trading posts along the western coast of Africa in the late fifteenth century. They traded with the local African rulers for slaves and African produce, such as gold, animal hides, and ivory. The demand for slaves grew rapidly from the sixteenth century onward, with the development of European colonies in the Americas.

Europeans in the Americas required slaves for their plantations and farms. Africans were accustomed to the tropical climate of the warmer regions of the Americas and were able to adapt to working in mines and on plantations. The Atlantic slave trade, which had started in low numbers in the fifteenth century, suddenly became important. At the height of the trade in the eighteenth century, some 45,000 Africans were transported across the Atlantic to the Americas each year.

Below: **A colored engraving depicts slaves being hauled aboard an Arab sailboat. The slaves would be transferred to larger European ships that would take the slaves across the Atlantic to the Americas.**

The Role of Nigerian Kingdoms

The kingdom of Benin was one of the most important slave markets west of the Niger River. Slaves were traded for foreign fabrics, brass armlets, mirrors, fine coral, beads, and perfumes. In return, the traders of Benin exported slaves, local cloth, pepper, jasper stones, leopard skins, and ivory. Many cities and towns of the delta region became wealthy through the trade in slaves.

Nearly one-third of the slaves brought to the Americas were exported through the Niger Delta ports of Bonny, Calabar, Badagary, and Lagos. Slaves captured on the mainland were transported by canoe or by foot to the coast, where they were sold to slave traders. Slave raids were carried out mostly by the Africans themselves. The slave raiders usually captured or took prisoners from rival ethnic groups. The slaves were transported across the Atlantic, chained in the cargo holds of ships. Conditions on board the ships were inhumane, and many Africans died during the long sea journeys. The Atlantic slave trade continued until 1888, when Brazil abolished slavery. Brazil was the last country in the Americas to do so.

SAMUEL AJAYI CROWTHER

In 1821, a young Nigerian boy was captured as a slave. He was sold to a Portuguese trader in Lagos and put on a ship bound for Brazil. The slaves were rescued by a British squadron and taken to Freetown in Sierra Leone. In Freetown, the boy attended a village school and was looked after by a European missionary. He returned with his guardian to Britain and converted to Christianity. He took the name Samuel Crowther. Crowther became the first Christian African clergyman and was sent to Nigeria. He made several journeys into the country's interior to preach Christianity. He also wrote many books and translated the Bible into Yoruba and other Nigerian languages. Crowther eventually became the first Bishop of Nigeria.

Tale of Two Cities

Lagos

Lagos is situated in the southwest region of Nigeria and was the country's capital until December 1991. The indigenous people of Lagos are Yorubas, but the city is cosmopolitan and inhabited by people from all ethnic groups. The largest city in Nigeria, Lagos has an estimated population of thirteen million. The city is acutely overcrowded, suffers from serious traffic congestion and a high crime rate, and has very little natural room for expansion. Successive governments since Nigeria's independence have tried to solve the problems of this growing city, but the Nigerian government finally decided that a new capital was needed.

In 1976, a government committee was set up to investigate the relocation of the country's capital. The idea was to build a capital city that would belong to all Nigerians — one that would symbolize unity. The committee's task was to find a centrally located area that had room for growth and little or no ethnic affiliations. After much discussion, Abuja was recommended. The area was roughly in the geographical center of the country. More importantly, Abuja was not within the territory of any one ethnic group.

Left: **Aso Rock is an important landmark in Abuja. The president's palace is located at its base.**

Above: **The offices of the Nigerian National Petroleum Corporation in Abuja are equipped with state-of-the-art security systems.**

Abuja

Abuja lies about 300 miles (480 km) northeast of Lagos. The journey from Abuja to Lagos takes eight hours by road and one hour by air. Abuja covers an area of 2,824 square miles (7,314 square km). Situated at an elevation of 1,180 feet (360 m) above sea level, the city has a cooler climate than Lagos, which is hot and humid. Other factors that make Abuja a more suitable capital than Lagos include the availability of a good supply of water and electricity, a network of roads that links Abuja to all parts of the country, and fertile soil that has a good natural drainage.

Building commenced in 1980. Government ministries and diplomatic missions moved to Abuja in 1990. Although Abuja was officially declared the new capital a year later, construction is still not quite complete.

Abuja is a beautiful city with few of the problems present in Lagos. The city is safe, well lit, and well laid out. Power blackouts are rare. Abuja, however, has its own share of problems. Housing is still insufficient, and rents are extremely high. On weekends, the city is empty because most people spend their weekends in Lagos, which remains the commercial hub of Nigeria.

Traditional Architecture

Nigerian buildings include more than mud huts. Many types of traditional architecture exist. Buildings evolved in response to the environment, culture, and politics, as well as to the availability of building materials and technology.

Shapes and Styles

Traditional Nigerian houses have one of five shapes — square, rectangle, circle, cylinder, or cone. In the mangrove forests, wood is plentiful. Wooden houses in the fishing communities here are built on stilts raised above the water level. Walls are made from wooden planks, and roofs from wood covered with thatch. Houses in the tropical areas and open savannas are usually built around a courtyard. Verandas are also common. In the north, houses also have courtyards but no verandas.

Above: **Men in Maiduguri use hay and earth to construct a traditional house.**

Buildings usually consist of wood structural posts or frames in a square or round formation, with straight or curved walls. Conical roofs are common. Windows usually face each other for ventilation. Steep, pitched roofs are common in areas with heavy rainfall. Roofs are not as steep in drier lands.

Below: **The interior of a Fulani bedroom in Sokoto is simple yet comfortable.**

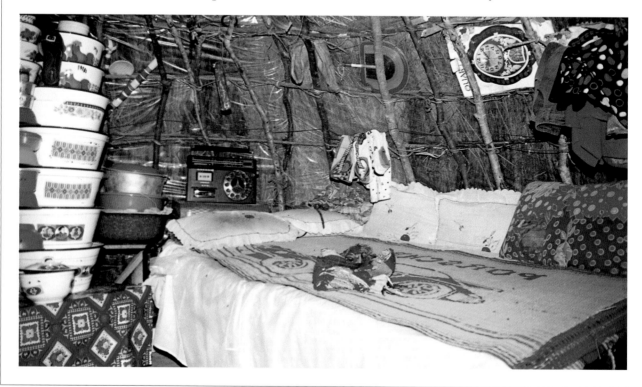

People sometimes build roofed terraces on which to relax during the cool evenings.

Above: **Houses in Kano have small distinctive towers at each corner.**

Building Materials

Building materials vary depending on an area's climate and vegetation. Generally, mud and clay are spread directly on walls or are first shaped into bricks. Granite and sandstone are also used. Timber in the form of hardwood, bamboo, and coconut palm trunks is used for structural posts.

Roofing materials include reeds, grass, and coconut palm leaves. In the north, thatch roofs once were common, but as the supply of grass decreased, other materials were used for roofing.

Influences

Europeans influenced the style and construction of some traditional buildings. Courtyards were abandoned, and concrete blocks, instead of mud, were used for walls. Thatch was replaced by corrugated aluminum, iron, or zinc sheets. Houses built during the colonial period generally have concrete block walls, wood frames, wood windows and doors, and corrugated zinc roofs. Most of these houses have verandas, patios, and large gardens.

MOSQUES

All mosques have the same basic design, but they differ in size and richness of detail. Ablution chambers, where believers wash their face, arms, and feet, lead to large, enclosed courtyards that are divided into three aisles. The prayer niche faces Mecca, toward which the faithful pray. Islam forbids the use of human representation in architecture, but calligraphy and decorative motifs are used extensively.

Yoruba Religion

Traditional Yoruba religion has a long history and predates the arrival of Christianity and Islam in Nigeria. This religion is still practiced today in Nigeria, as well as in the Americas by descendants of Nigerians who arrived during the slave trade.

Like Christians and Muslims, followers of traditional Yoruba religion believe in the existence of an almighty God, whom they call *Olorun* (oh-law-ROON). They accept Olorun as maker of heaven and Earth but consider him too majestic and too divine to be approached directly by man. To reach him, the people use intermediaries, or deities known as *orishas* (oh-REE-shahs).

Followers worship these deities and communicate through them with the supreme being.

The Yoruba creation myth places a town called Ife at the center of the origin of mankind. Traditional Yorubas believe that in the beginning, Earth was covered with water. The supreme creator, Olorun, sent his son Oduduwa down a gold chain carrying some soil, a cockerel, and a palm kernel. Oduduwa scattered the soil over the water. The cockerel then scratched the soil and placed the palm kernel into the soil. An oil palm grew, marking the site of Ife, which is still revered today as the cradle of civilization and the Yoruba race.

Above: **Figures of hunters and priests adorn this roadside Yoruba shrine in Ife. Religious art is an important part of traditional religion.**

Ogun

Ogun (oh-GOON) is the Yoruba god of war. All instruments and objects made of iron are symbols of Ogun. According to Yoruba oral tradition, Ogun was the first son of Oduduwa, who is considered a mythical common ancestor of the Yorubas. Ogun was a great warrior who waged successful military battles. He is traditionally worshiped by soldiers, blacksmiths, and men or women whose livelihoods are related to war or objects of iron.

Ifa

Ifa (EE-fah) is believed to be a great oracle consulted before the installation of a ruler. No important enterprise is undertaken without the blessing or approval of Ifa. In addition to telling the

Below: **This building near Oshogbo is a shrine to Oshun, the river goddess of fertility and abundance.**

future, the priests who honor Ifa also diagnose diseases. A long course of serious study and apprenticeship is necessary in order to become an Ifa priest.

Sango

Historically, *Sango* (SHAN-go) was a Yoruba king. In his lifetime, he was powerful, good, and fair. The visible signs of Sango are lightning and thunder. When a building or person is struck by lightning, Yorubas believe Sango is expressing his displeasure for some sin or offense. The symbols of Sango are smooth stones shaped like an ax head. These stones represent thunder.

RELATIONS WITH NORTH AMERICA

Relations between Nigeria and North America have experienced many ups and downs over the years. With Nigerian independence in 1960, the American Consulate in Lagos was upgraded to an embassy, and relations between Nigeria and the United States reached a new and significant phase.

The United States today recognizes Nigeria as one of the most important countries in Africa because of its large population and vast economic resources. Many opportunities exist for the development of mutual trade between Nigeria and the United

Opposite: **Nigerian-born Houston Rockets center Hakeem Olajuwon (*left*) tries to pass the ball during a game against the Los Angeles Clippers at the Compaq Center in Houston in 1999.**

States, and government and business leaders of both countries are eager to build strong economic and political ties.

Cultural links between the two countries are strong because of the many African-Americans who are descended from Nigerians brought over to the United States as slaves. Many Nigerians come to the United States for higher education. Nigeria's first president, Nnamdi Azikiwe, attended Lincoln and Colombia universities. Nigerian customs, food, and music are popular among African-Americans, while American pop music is a favorite with Nigerian youths living in the large cities.

Above: **U.S. president Bill Clinton greets villagers in Ushafa, Niger State, during his official visit to Nigeria in 2000.**

1960s and 1970s

In the 1960s and 1970s, Nigeria was an important focus of U.S. and Soviet foreign policy because of its large population, military capabilities, and oil reserves. The Soviet Union provided military equipment to Nigeria during the Biafran War (1967–1970), while the United States, although officially neutral, supported the Biafran government.

After the war, Nigeria became more important to the United States because of Nigeria's increasing oil revenues and because the United States realized Nigeria was a strategic African power.

1980s and 1990s

The early 1980s, however, saw relations between the two nations plunge. Links between the Reagan administration (1981–1989) and the apartheid (racial segregation) regime in South Africa soured relations between Nigeria and the United States. Many Nigerians were unhappy that the United States condoned apartheid and continued to trade with South Africa.

During the Persian Gulf War in 1991, Nigeria supported the action of the United Nations and the United States to invade Iraq. Nigeria's support, plus racial reforms in South Africa, helped mend relations between Nigeria and the United States.

Above: **Biafran soldiers man a jeep mounted with a machine gun during the Biafran civil war in eastern Nigeria.**

Below: **Some oil refineries in Port Harcourt were set on fire after the Nigerian army captured the town from Biafran rebel forces in May 1968.**

Left: **Nigerian president Olusegun Obasanjo (*left*) shakes hands with U.S. president Bill Clinton during Obasanjo's visit to the United States in October 1999.**

In 1993, however, relations between the two countries once again took a downward turn. The unsuccessful Nigerian presidential election that year and a series of human rights abuses under General Sani Abacha's military regime (1993–1998) led the United States to impose trade restrictions on Nigeria. Direct airplane flights between Lagos and U.S. cities were also suspended. Tensions increased further in 1995, when the U.S. ambassador was recalled for four months following the execution of Ken Saro-Wiwa and eight other Ogoni activists.

The situation changed dramatically in May 1999, when a new, democratically elected government came to power in Nigeria. Since then, relations between Nigeria and the United States have improved significantly. In an effort to support Nigeria's transition to democracy, the Clinton administration (1992–2000) declared Nigeria one of the primary recipients of United States monetary aid. In October 1999, Nigerian president Olusegun Obasanjo visited the United States as part of a world tour to restore confidence in Nigeria. United States president Bill Clinton returned the visit in August 2000, when he paid an official state visit to Nigeria, the first by a U.S. president in over twenty years.

Economic Relations

Today, the economic links between the United States and Nigeria are stronger than they have ever been since Nigeria's independence. The United States is Nigeria's largest trading partner. Nigeria is the United States' largest trading partner on the African continent and supplies 8 percent of all oil imported into the United States. Two-way trade between the countries exceeds U.S. $10 billion annually.

The United States exports a wide variety of commodities to Nigeria, including energy equipment, computers, wheat, and shipping equipment. Nigerian exports to the United States are largely crude oil and petroleum products. Both countries now wish to expand export opportunities. Corporations in the United States have gradually become more interested in doing business with African companies. They believe Nigeria is a profitable market because of its large population. Large American businesses operating in Nigeria today include the oil giant Chevron.

Above: **Legislators at the National Assembly of Nigeria in Abuja rise to greet U.S. president Bill Clinton during his official visit to Nigeria in 2000.**

Concrete Economic Steps

The United States Congress recently enacted the African Growth and Opportunity Act, a bill intended to increase trade between the United States and sub-Saharan Africa. The act allows African economies greater access to U.S. markets. Nigeria in particular is expected to benefit since it is the largest market in Africa for U.S. goods. The act could result in significant employment growth and the transfer of capital and technology to Nigeria, especially in the textile and manufacturing industries.

The U.S.–Nigeria Trade and Investment Council was inaugurated in June 2000, with the aim of expanding trade between Nigeria and the United States. The council also aims to implement policies that promote economic growth in Nigeria and reduce the country's dependence on oil. The council is part of the U.S. government's growth- and trade-oriented approach toward developing countries in sub-Saharan Africa.

Yet another organization expanding business opportunities between Nigeria and the United States is the Joint Economic Partnership Committee, which was set up in Washington D.C. in November 1999. This economic forum is an opportunity for the governments of both countries to forge long-term economic partnerships through dialogue.

Below: **Former U.S. ambassador to the United Nations Andrew Young (*right*) applauds President Bill Clinton after Clinton's speech at the National Summit on Africa in Washington D.C. in 2000.**

Strong Cultural Ties

Cultural ties between Americans and Nigerians go back hundreds of years because of the slave trade. Many African-Americans visit Nigeria to trace their roots. They visit Nigeria's coastal towns, where they can still see chains and neck irons once used in the slave trade. Some African-Americans have even moved to Nigeria.

Traditional Nigerian clothes have become popular with African-Americans. These clothes include the dansiki, aso oke cloth, and traditional printed shirts. Nigerian influence can also be seen in modern American dance. The Dance Theater of Harlem, a New York-based ballet company, blends classical ballet with the rich heritage of African and African-American dance. Yoruba and Igbo dances, in particular, are popular choices for adaptation to contemporary American dance performances.

American culture in Nigeria has influenced many areas of life, from banking and commerce to ordinary speech, music, and food. Many city-dwelling Nigerians have access to satellite television. Nigerian youth culture is strongly influenced by broadcasts from U.S. channels. Many Nigerians also choose to study at U.S. universities. A number of Nigerian restaurants in Lagos and other large cities model themselves on U.S. fast-food chains, such as Kentucky Fried Chicken and McDonald's.

OYOTUNJI VILLAGE

Almost thirty years ago, African-American dancer Walter Eugene King set up Oyotunji African Village near Charleston in South Carolina. Based on Yoruba culture, Oyotunji attracts visitors eager to see authentic Yoruba dancing, religious festivals, and a traditional Yoruba market. Many African-Americans live in the village, dressing in traditional Yoruba style and even speaking the Yoruba language.

Below: The Dance Theater of Harlem performs ballets inspired by traditional Nigerian dance.

Above: **Nigerian-Americans in New York dressed in traditional Nigerian clothes march in a parade marking the fortieth year of Nigerian independence.**

Immigration

During the Biafran civil war, the United States accepted many Igbo refugees who were affected by the fighting. Some of these people have remained in the United States, raising new generations of African-Americans. Today, Nigerians continue to immigrate to the United States, and they make up a significant proportion of people entering the United States via the Diversity Visa Lottery. This lottery allows people from certain countries the opportunity to immigrate to the United States. New immigrants from Nigeria are often highly qualified professionals who integrate successfully into U.S. society.

Nigerians who have become U.S. citizens retain their links with their home country, and many visit Nigeria at least once a year. Nigerians in the United States often set up clubs to keep in touch with each other. Nigerian citizens who work in the United States often send money home to Nigeria. The money is then used to build houses or start businesses in their villages. This is a traditional practice for many Nigerians living abroad.

Nigerians in Canada

Canada is home to many Nigerians and Canadians of Nigerian descent. Nigerian-Canadians have established numerous associations and clubs. These organizations include the Association of Northern Nigerians in Canada and the Yoruba Community Association. The groups promote Nigerian culture in Canada and maintain close links with communities in Nigeria. Members gather frequently for picnics and carnivals, as well as to celebrate Nigerian festivals and independence day. The umbrella organization for Nigerian clubs in Canada is the Nigerian Canadian Association, which is based in Toronto.

Prominent Nigerian-Canadians include wrestler Daniel Igali. He was the 1999 world champion wrestler in the 152-pound (69-kg) free style class. A year later, Igali won the gold medal in the same category at the 2000 Olympic Games in Sydney, earning Canada's first Olympic gold medal in wrestling. Igali was born in Port Harcourt in 1974 and moved to Canada in 1994, where he attended Simon Fraser University.

Above: **At the 2000 Olympic Games in Sydney, Nigerian-Canadian Daniel Igali won Canada's first Olympic gold medal in the sport of wrestling.**

The Peace Corps in Nigeria

Formed in 1961 in the United States, the Peace Corps sent approximately 1,800 volunteers to Nigeria, mainly during the 1960s. American volunteers assisted in various projects in health care, community development, agriculture, and education.

During the 1970s and 1980s, no Peace Corps volunteers were sent to Nigeria, mainly because of the political unrest in the country. The Peace Corps resumed sending volunteers to Nigeria in the early 1990s, but stopped in 1995, again as a result of the unstable political situation. During his historic visit to Nigeria in August 2000, U.S. president Bill Clinton said that the Peace Corps planned to bring back volunteers to Nigeria.

Peace Corps volunteers who served in Nigeria have set up Friends of Nigeria, an organization that serves to keep former volunteers in touch with one another. Friends of Nigeria also seeks to educate ordinary Americans about Nigeria and promotes continued service to the Nigerian people. Many Nigerians living in the United States are also members of the organization. Friends of Nigeria produces newsletters in which former volunteers describe their experiences during service as Peace Corps volunteers in Nigeria.

AN AMERICAN IN NIGERIA

Yeye Olade was born Michele Paul in Denver in 1944. At the age of sixteen, she decided she would move to Africa one day. In 1978, she and her family flew to Nigeria and settled in a rural Yoruba village. Paul changed her name to Yeye, which means "mother" in the Yoruba language. Today, she lives in Oyo State and is the chief librarian of the African Heritage Research Library, the first rural-based African studies library in Africa.

A NIGERIAN IN AMERICA

Phillip Emeagwali is an outstanding Nigerian-American who was described by U.S. president Bill Clinton as one of the great minds of the information age. He developed a computer capable of making 3.1 billion calculations per second. Emeagwali grew up in Onitsha and is now a consultant in Baltimore.

Left: Phillip Emeagwali poses beside his invention — a formula that calculates the rate at which crude oil is pumped up from the ground.

Sport

Some of Nigeria's talented athletes live in the United States. One of the most famous Nigerian-American sportsmen is Hakeem Olajuwon, more popularly known as "Akeem the Dream." This seven-footer, who currently plays basketball for the Houston Rockets, was born in Lagos in 1963. He studied at the University of Houston in the United States. He left college when he was selected by a professional basketball team, the Houston Rockets, to play center in 1984. His basketball career has been marked by many awards, including the 1999 National Basketball Association's (NBA) Sportsmanship Award.

Above: **Hakeem Olajuwon (*left*) attempts to gain control of the ball.**

Another famous U.S. basketball player of Nigerian descent is Michael Olowokandi, who was also born in Lagos. Olowokandi plays for the Los Angles Clippers and is a rising star in the NBA.

Nigerian and American athletes often compete against one other in international sporting events. At the 2000 Olympic Games in Sydney, Nigeria won a silver medal in the men's 1,600-meter relay, just behind the United States. The Nigerian women's 1,600-meter relay team finished three places behind their U.S. counterparts. Another clash between the two countries came in the women's 100-meter hurdles, when Nigerian hurdler Glory Alozie claimed an Olympic silver medal, ahead of American Melissa Morrison, who finished in third place.

Below: **Nigerian hurdler Glory Alozie (*left*) thunders past American Sharon Crouch in the semifinal heats of the 100-meter women's hurdles, at the Sydney 2000 Olympic Games.**

Nigerians in Hollywood

Nigerian actors have made their mark in the world of U.S. television and film production. Nigerian actors Maynard Eziashi, Bella Enahoro, and Ariyon Bakare appeared in the 1991 film *Mr. Johnson* opposite actor Pierce Brosnan. The story is set in colonial Nigeria of the 1930s and portrays the complex issue of human identity in a rapidly changing world. Eziashi also starred with Jim Carrey in the comedy *Ace Ventura: When Nature Calls* (1995), playing the role of a young African prince.

Edafe Blackmon is a rising Nigerian-American actor who has a regular acting role on the romantic situation comedy *For Your Love*, produced by Warner Brothers. He plays the dashing playboy Reggie Ellis. Blackmon was born in Washington D.C., but he spent part of his childhood in Lagos, where he attended elementary school. He was first noticed in the critically acclaimed television movie *And the Band Played On* (1993), which featured, among others, Matthew Modine, Richard Gere, and Angelica Huston. Blackmon also has guest-starred in television shows, including *Hangin' with Mr. Cooper* and *A Different World*.

Above: **Kirk Douglas (***right***) has a friendly spar with Nigerian boxer Hogan "Kid" Bassey (***left***) on the set of** *Spartacus* **(1960). The Nigerian boxing superstar is said to have given Douglas a few tips on hand-to-hand combat.**

NIGERIA

Map labels:

NIGER

S A H A R A   D E S E R T

CHA

Lake Chad

□1 ● Sokoto
● Argungu
S
□2
□3
● Katsina
A
H
□4 ● Kano
● Zaria
□6
□5
E
□7
L
□8 ● Ngazargamu
● Maiduguri
Nguru Wetlands

BENIN

□11
□10 ● Ushafa
Kainji Lake
Borgu Game Reserve
Kainji Dam
● Kaduna
Kaduna
□12 ● Kumo
□13
● Nok
Jos ● Nok
Jos Plateau
Gongola
Yankari National Park
Bende
□14 ● Mubi
Chappal Waddi (7,936 ft/2,419 m)
● Yola
● Koma
Loh Mountains
CHAD

□9
■ ABUJA
□19
□20
□21
□22
CAMEROON

□15
Ogun
● Ilorin
□18
Benue
Lokoja ●
● Makurdi
□28
Katsina

Ogbomosho ●
□23 ● Oyo
● Ibadan
□16 ● Oshogbo
● Ife
□17
● Abeokuta
Omo Forest Reserve
□26
□25
□24 ● Badagary
● Lagos
● Benin City
□27 ● Nsukka
□29 ● Enugu
□30
Onitsha
● Asaba ●
□32
□31
□33
Cross River
Cross River National Park
□34
Afi River Forest Reserve
Obudu Cattle Ranch
Mbe Mountains
Oban Hills

Gulf of Guinea

□36
□35
□37 ● Uyo
Oban Hills
● Calabar
Port Harcourt
● Opobo
● Bonny
Niger Delta
South Atlantic Ocean

N

Legend:
—	State Boundary
■	Capital
●	City
～	River
✳	Dam

STATES

1 SOKOTO	9 KWARA	17 EKITI	24 LAGOS	32 IMO
2 KEBBI	10 NIGER	18 KOGI	25 ONDO	33 ABIA
3 ZAMFARA	11 KADUNA	19 ABUJA FEDERAL CAPITAL TERRITORY	26 EDO	34 CROSS RIVER
4 KATSINA	12 BAUCHI		27 ENUGU	35 BAYELSA
5 KANO	13 GOMBE	20 NASSARAWA	28 BENUE	36 RIVERS
6 JIGAWA	14 ADAMAWA	21 PLATEAU	29 ANAMBRA	37 AKWA IBOM
7 YOBE	15 OYO	22 TARABA	30 EBONYI	
8 BORNO	16 OSUN	23 OGUN	31 DELTA	

Above: Lagos is a bustling modern city that looks out over the Atlantic Ocean.

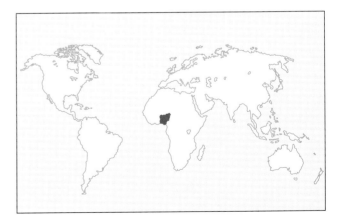

NIGERIA

How Is Your Geography?

Learning to identify the main geographical areas and points of a country can be challenging. Although it may seem difficult at first to memorize the locations and spellings of major cities or the names of mountain ranges, rivers, deserts, lakes, and other prominent physical features, the end result of this effort can be very rewarding. Places you previously did not know existed will suddenly come to life when referred to in world news, whether in newspapers, television reports, or other books and reference sources. This knowledge will make you feel a bit closer to the rest of the world, with its fascinating variety of cultures and physical geography.

Used in a classroom setting, the instructor can make duplicates of this map using a copy machine. (PLEASE DO NOT WRITE IN THIS BOOK!) Students can then fill in any requested information on their individual map copies. Used one-on-one, the student can also make copies of the map on a copy machine and use them as a study tool. The student can practice identifying place names and geographical features on his or her own.

Above: **These villagers live in small communities along the Niger River near Onitsha.**

Nigeria at a Glance

Official Name   Federal Republic of Nigeria

Capital   Abuja

Official Language   English

Native Languages   Hausa, Yoruba, Igbo, Fulfulde

Population   123.3 million (2000 estimate)

Land Area   356,700 square miles (923,853 square km)

States   Abia, Abuja Federal Capital Territory, Adamawa, Akwa Ibom, Anambra, Bauchi, Bayelsa, Benue, Borno, Cross River, Delta, Ebonyi, Edo, Ekiti, Enugu, Gombe, Imo, Jigawa, Kaduna, Kano, Katsina, Kebbi, Kogi, Kwara, Lagos, Nassarawa, Niger, Ogun, Ondo, Osun, Oyo, Plateau, Rivers, Sokoto, Taraba, Yobe, Zamfara

Highest Point   Chappal Waddi 7,936 feet (2,419 m)

Major Rivers   Benue, Cross, Gongola, Kaduna, Niger, Ogun, Sokoto

Major Lakes   Chad, Kainji

Famous Leaders   Abubakar Tafawa Balewa (1912–1966); Nnamdi Azikiwe (1904–1996)

Major Cities   Abuja, Ibadan, Kano, Lagos, Port Harcourt

Main Religions   Islam, Christianity, African traditional religions

Major Imports   Building material, chemicals, live animals, machinery, manufactured goods, transportation equipment

Major Exports   Cocoa, oil and petroleum products, rubber, tin

Major Festivals   National Day (October 1)

Id al-Fitri (December)

Currency   Nigerian Naira (NGN 112.45 = U.S. $1 in 2001)

Opposite: **This painting by famous Nigerian artist Jimoh Buraimoh is entitled** *Masquerade.*

Glossary

Nigerian Vocabulary

agbada (ahg-BAH-dah): a loose, flowing gown worn by Yoruba men.

agidigbo (ah-GEE-DIG-boh): a thumb piano made from a piece of wood with metal strips; a style of music featuring this instrument accompanied by drumming.

akara (ah-KAH-rah): a fried snack made from beans.

akwete (ah-KWAY-tay): a cloth produced by Igbos in southeastern Nigeria.

aso oke (AH-soh oh-kay): a cloth woven by Yorubas in southwestern Nigeria.

ayo (AH-yo): an African board game.

boubou (BOO-boo): a robe for women.

buba (BOO-bah): a short-sleeved tunic.

dansiki (dahn-SEE-kee): a traditional loose tunic, worn with loose trousers.

darra (DAH-rah): the Hausa name for *ayo*.

dash (DAHSH): a gift or tip

dundun (DOON-doon): hourglass-shaped drums played with a drum stick.

eba (EE-bah): a paste made from tapioca.

egusi (ee-GOO-see): a hot, spicy stew.

ehi (AY-hee): personal gods of the citizens of ancient Benin.

Id al-Fitri (EED ahl-FIT-ree): Islamic festival held at the end of the Ramadan month of fasting.

Ifa (EE-fah): oracle in the Yoruba religion.

igbin (IG-been): a Yoruba dance.

Igue (ee-GOO-ay): new year's festival in Benin City.

Ikeji (ee-KAY-jee): Igbo masquerade.

jollof (JAW-lof): a dish made with rice, tomatoes, and meat.

juju (JOO-joo): a fusion of Yoruba and American musical styles.

kokoma (koh-koh-MAH): a musical style characterized by heavy drumming.

korokoro (KOH-roh-KOH-roh): a dance form based on martial art.

kulikuli (KOO-lee-KOO-lee): a snack made of small balls of peanut paste.

kulle (KEW-luh): the traditional Islamic practice of wife-seclusion.

lappa (LAH-pah): a piece of cloth wrapped around the waist.

moyin-moyin (MOH-yeen-MOH-yeen): steamed cakes of black-eyed beans.

oba (OH-bah): the ruler of ancient Benin.

Oduduwa (oh-doo-DOO-ah): the mythical ancestor of the Yoruba people.

Ogun (oh-GOON): the Yoruba god of war.

okwe (OH-kway): the Igbo name for *ayo*.

Olorun (oh-law-ROON): the Yoruba supreme being.

orishas (oh-REE-shahs): Yoruba deities.

Osanobua (oh-san-oh-BOO-ah): the supreme being in ancient Benin belief.

Oshun (oh-SHOON): Yoruba river deity.

purdah (PURR-dah): veiling of the face.

sallah (SAH-lah): a ceremony saluting the traditional emirs, or rulers, of the north.

Sango (SHAN-goh): the Yoruba god of thunder and lightning.

Shari'a (SHAH-ree-yah): Islamic law.

sokoto (so-KOH-toe): loose and tapered men's trousers.

suya (SOO-yah): spicy meat kabobs.

tuwo (TOO-woh): a paste made from millet, corn, or rice.

English Vocabulary

activist: someone who works vigorously for a cause.

affiliations: links; associations.

animism: the belief that natural objects possess spirits.

appease: to calm or pacify.

apprenticeship: a period of work or study under a master craftsperson.

autonomous: independent; self-governing.

baobab: a large, tropical African tree.

biodiversity: the variety of plant and animal species in an environment.

calabashes: dried-out gourds.

charismatic: describing Christian groups that seek an emotional religious experience through prayer and singing.

charter: a set of rules and regulations.

columbite: a black mineral consisting mostly of metallic elements.

corrugated: evenly wrinkled or folded.

coup d'état: a political action leading to a sudden change of government.

diagnose: to determine the identity of a disease by a medical examination.

diversify: to expand into different areas.

ecosystem: a community of organisms and its environment functioning together as a unit.

effigies: images or representations, especially of people.

eloquence: the ability to use language fluently in writing and speaking.

emir: a traditional leader in an Islamic country.

endemic: native to a particular region.

Establishment: people and institutions constituting the existing power structure in society.

evangelical: describing a Christian denomination that interprets the Bible in a conservative way.

facades: the fronts of buildings.

fray: show signs of wearing out.

freight: cargo that is being transported.

grass-roots: pertaining to ordinary citizens.

hydroelectricity: electricity derived from the energy of falling water.

indigenous: occurring naturally in a particular place.

indiscriminate: lacking in care or judgment.

irrigation: the act of supplying land with water by artificial means.

looting: the act of stealing, especially during wars or civil strife.

mangrove: a tree of the family *Rhizophora* that grows on marshy shores.

masquerades: festive gatherings of people wearing masks and costumes.

migratory: roving; wandering.

nomadic: roaming from place to place.

oracle: a deity that answers questions about the future.

pastoralists: farmers.

plantains: starchy, bananalike fruits.

plastography: the art of molding figures out of plastic materials.

Sahel: an arid region south of the Sahara Desert that stretches across six countries from Senegal to Chad.

subsistence: having the minimum of food and shelter necessary to support life.

tapioca: a granular form of cassava, a nutritious starchy plant.

torsos: the trunks of human bodies.

verandas: porches extending across the front and sides of houses.

More Books to Read

Ancient African Town. Picture a Country series. Fiona MacDonald (Franklin Watts)

Benin: Lords of the River. The Kingdoms of Africa series. Philip Koslow (Chelsea House)

The Kingdom of Benin. First Book series. Dominique Malaquais (Franklin Watts)

The Kingdom of Benin in West Africa. Cultures of the Past series. Heather Millar (Benchmark Books)

Nigeria. Cultures of the World series. Patricia Marjorie Levy (Benchmark Books)

Nigeria. Economically Developing Countries series. Alasdair Tenquist (Thomson Learning)

Nigeria. Festivals of the World series. Elizabeth Berg (Gareth Stevens)

Nigeria. Major World Nations series. Nicholas Freville (Chelsea House)

Nigeria: 1880 to the Present: The Struggle, the Tragedy, the Promise. Exploration of Africa: The Emerging Nations series. Daniel E. Harmon (Chelsea House)

Nigeria the Culture. Lands, Peoples, and Cultures series. Anne Rosenberg and Bobbie Kalman (Crabtree)

Nigeria in Pictures. Visual Geography series. Thomas O'Toole (Lerner)

Nigeria: A Nation of Many Peoples. Discovering our Heritage series. John Owhonda (Dillon Press)

Videos

Africa: The Story of a Continent. Programs 03-04. (Home Vision Cinema)

Foreign Correspondent — Nigeria: The Long Road to Democracy. (ABC Videos)

Web Sites

www.nigeriannation.com/nigeria/folk_tales/folk_tales.asp

cghs.dade.k12.fl.us/african-american/tradtional/nok.htm

www.motherlandnigeria.com/kidzone.html

Due to the dynamic nature of the Internet, some web sites stay current longer than others. To find additional web sites, use a reliable search engine with one or more of the following keywords to help you locate information about Nigeria. Keywords: *Abuja, Argungu Fishing Festival, Igbo, Lagos, Nigerians, Nok culture, Ben Okri, Yoruba.*

Index